CAMBRIDGE International E

Professional Development for Teachers

Teaching and Assessing Practical Skills in
Science

Dave Hayward

CAMBRIDGE
UNIVERSITY PRESS

PUBLISHED BY THE PRESS SYNDICATE OF THE UNIVERSITY OF CAMBRIDGE
The Pitt Building, Trumpington Street, Cambridge, United Kingdom

CAMBRIDGE UNIVERSITY PRESS
The Edinburgh Building, Cambridge CB2 2RU, UK
40 West 20th Street, New York, NY 10011-4211, USA
477 Williamstown Road, Port Melbourne, VIC 3207, Australia
Ruiz de Alarcón 13, 28014 Madrid, Spain
Dock House, The Waterfront, Cape Town 8001, South Africa

http://www.cambridge.org

First published 2003

Printed in the United Kingdom at the University Press, Cambridge

Typefaces Meridien, Dax condensed *System* QuarkXPress®

A catalogue record for this book is available from the British Library

ISBN 0 521 75359 7 paperback

The photographs in the book are reproduced courtesy of Dave Hayward.

The publisher has used its best endeavours to ensure that the URLs for external websites
referred to in this book are correct and active at the time of going to press. However, the
publisher has no responsibility for the websites and can make no guarantee that a site will
remain live or that the content will remain appropriate.

Contents

For Kath

Foreword

Teaching is a complex and demanding profession. All over the world, societies change in response to new knowledge gained, technological developments, globalisation and a requirement for an ever-more sophisticated and educated population. Teachers are in the forefront of such social change, responding with speed and confidence to the new demands made of them, in terms of both their knowledge and the way in which they teach. This series is intended to help them in their adaptation to change and in their professional development as teachers.

Curriculum changes worldwide are putting increased emphasis on the acquisition of skills as well as subject knowledge, so that students will have the ability to respond flexibly to the swiftly changing modern environment. As a result, teachers must be able both to teach and assess skills and to adjust their own teaching methods to embrace a wider range of techniques for both teaching and assessing in the classroom. The books in this series are practical handbooks which explore these techniques and offer advice on how to use them to enhance the teacher's own practice.

The handbooks are written by teachers with direct experience of teaching and assessing skills at this level. We have asked them to write for their readers in such a way that the readers feel directly supported in their professional development. Thus, as well as tasks for students, there are tasks for teachers, pauses for reflection and questions to be answered. We hope that readers will find that this mixture of the practical and the professional helps them, both in their practice and in their own sense of what it means to be an effective teacher in this modern, changing world of international education.

Dr Kate Pretty
Series Editor

Acknowledgements

I am thankful to Dr Allison Cook for her helpful Physics contributions, to Elaine Wilson for her constructive suggestions and to Camilla Erskine – a source of gentle encouragement and support.

Photographs and ideas have been produced and developed with the help of students and technicians at Spennymoor School, County Durham – a great place to work and learn.

1 Introduction

The purpose and contents of the book

The pressures of time, limited resources and the need to enable students to achieve the best possible results affect most of us as Science teachers. The result can be that we concentrate on the theory contained within the syllabus we use, to the detriment of all but the minimum practical work to get students through that part of the course. However, teaching is about much more than preparing students for examinations. Practical work is essential in enabling students to gain first-hand experience of phenomena. It stimulates curiosity and interest in the subject, helping to develop enquiring minds that want to explore more, offering challenges to existing beliefs.

Where will future scientists come from if we do not inspire our students through experience of practical science – enabling them to see how accepted scientific concepts and bodies of knowledge were discovered, running experiments to produce data to support the theory found in textbooks and giving them the opportunity to develop the skills to carry out original research themselves? Through their own investigative work, they can apply their conceptual understanding in new contexts. Admittedly, some students thrive on theory and we have a challenging job to do in bringing this to life and making it understandable. However, the majority have a range of different preferred learning styles that can only be accessed successfully through hands-on experience – practical work. Nevertheless, it is worth noting that any practical work needs to be thought provoking. Following a list of instructions without understanding the reasons for each stage achieves very little, except to keep students busy. That is not what practical work should be about. Examples are given later in the book of how students can be challenged to think about why they carry out a particular procedure (see, for example, Chapter 6, Table 6.1 – a strategy for building an understanding of how to test a leaf for starch). Other areas of practical work, such as planning, interpreting data, concluding and evaluating, require much thought: these thought processes will develop in your students as they are exposed to more practicals. The most effective Science teaching operates seamlessly between exploring abstract concepts, illustrative practical tasks, open-ended investigations and teacher-led demonstrations. Any Science lesson should offer constant challenges to get students thinking about all aspects of the topic they are studying.

There are many arguments for and against practical work, considered in Chapter 2. I have written this book to act as a stimulus for you to think carefully about how you approach your teaching, to provide you with ways of generating a real interest in and thirst for Science amongst your students and as a means of sharing experiences so that we all benefit through keeping our teaching fresh. After teaching Science for 23 years, it would be very easy for me to think that I know it all, that my teaching is as good as it is going to get and that work is now plain sailing through to retirement. Well, it isn't. It never ceases to amaze and delight me that a new student, fresh from university, can start a teaching practice in my department and show me methods of teaching a particular concept in ways I had never thought of. Textbooks appear on the market, dealing with topics that have never been considered in print before. Colleagues teaching a different subject area can come up with suggestions over a cup of tea about how to approach a subject that I find difficult to put across to a class. Teaching Science is never boring. We just need the impetus (and energy!) to keep trying out different ways of teaching. So, whether you have just embarked on a teaching career or have been teaching for several years, this book should provide you with some fresh ideas to make practicals interesting, challenging and exciting for your students. Once you are working towards that goal, everything else is more likely to fall into place amongst your students: high performance in examinations, respect for you as a teacher and a lifelong fascination for the subject.

Sharing is absolutely vital. If you generate a new resource that you find is successful, do not keep it to yourself. Swap ideas, sources and resources with others. Your colleagues are more likely to reciprocate and you should benefit as well. Try to encourage discussions in your own department. Fresh ideas do not necessarily have to come from within your own subject area – as a biologist, I have gained countless ideas from chemists and physicists and have contributed to the development of their practical teaching skills as well. Many practical skills are common to all three areas of Science, so this is hardly surprising.

How often do you get the chance to observe the teaching styles of your colleagues? I firmly believe in an open-door approach to my teaching – anyone is welcome to come into my laboratory, observe me and contribute to my teaching. As a Head of Department, I have roles in supporting the professional development of colleagues and observing student teachers as they embark on teacher training programmes. This is most definitely a two-way process – I gain as much as I give. Have you considered asking your Head Teacher for some time to allow you to observe other members of staff teaching, including those from other curriculum areas, particularly humanities teaching? The experience is invaluable. Too often we teach in total isolation and, in the process, are starved of fresh ideas, different approaches and strategies.

In this book, I have tried to use real examples of students' results, graphs, conclusions and evaluations to raise points about aspects of practical work. Because they are genuine, they are rarely perfect. I offer material from the real world, imperfect as it is – I prefer it that way. This is how it is in authentic scientific research. 'Messy data' challenges thinking! As these materials stand, they offer numerous points to dwell on, both for you as a teacher and, if you wish to use them as a teaching resource, for your students. Let them study the tables and graphs, pick holes in them and try to suggest improvements. Allow them to try to replicate the experiments, controlling the variables as they see fit to obtain a 'better' set of results. They will become more proficient, enthusiastic Science students as a result.

This book is divided into three parts. Chapters 2 and 3 look at the role of practical work in Science, considering its advantages and disadvantages and planning issues, respectively. Chapter 4 outlines the practical skills associated with Science, and Chapters 5 to 11 then look at each of these skills in turn. Finally, Chapter 12 looks at how to assess these skills, including the consideration of which syllabus option to select. There are four appendices. Details of useful sources of information – books, CD-ROMs, professional bodies and websites – can be found in Appendix A. The glossary in Appendix B defines terms that may need clarification, but it does not contain definitions of technical terms in Science. Appendix C provides lists of standard apparatus. Finally, Appendix D contains photocopiable worksheets – these can be enlarged to provide A4 worksheets.

The international education context

During my time (some 13 years now) associated with examining for the International General Certificate of Secondary Education (IGCSE) and in my role as a Principal Examiner, it has been pleasing to see the rise in popularity of Science courses on offer, perhaps partly due to uncluttered syllabuses and the availability of support from professional staff who offer helpful advice. I never cease to be impressed by the number of candidates who use English as a second, or even third, language and yet cope with the rigours of reading and writing extended English. I hope that, through this book, I have demonstrated that teachers can, even in the most challenging circumstances, use practical work as an invaluable way of engaging students and developing their knowledge and understanding of the subject. It should provide you with the guidance and support to extend your own practical skills, perhaps giving you the confidence to try different or new approaches to your teaching.

2 Practical work in Science

The word 'Science' originally meant 'knowledge'. Even now, it is applied to a wide range of disciplines including political science and the science of philosophy. However, in schools its use tends to be in grouping together three closely linked subjects – Biology, Chemistry and Physics. As teachers, we are well aware that the study of Science involves much more than just the gaining of knowledge (accumulating facts and principles). Any syllabus emphasises the need for students to understand the knowledge they learn, to be able to apply that knowledge to interpret information that is unfamiliar to them, to explain phenomena, patterns and relationships and to solve problems.

Indeed, the body of knowledge that we call Science has been built up over the centuries through observation, investigation and experimentation. As Science teachers, we have a duty to teach students the skills they need to be the scientists of the future. They will, of course, require a sound body of knowledge, but will also need to have the practical skills to extend humankind's understanding of the world around us, whether it be associated with physical phenomena, materials or living things. For any student, a Science course should be a worthwhile educational experience that is stimulating and challenging, enables the development of new skills and encourages effective communication. All students should learn Science to enable them to make informed decisions as citizens of the twenty-first century. They need to be informed about the controversial issues of Science so they can make balanced judgements about them. For others, learning Science will prepare them for their future role as scientists.

All of the sciences, therefore, have an essentially practical basis. The body of scientific knowledge that students learn in secondary schools has been built up through observation and experiment. It is important that, as well as teaching our students this body of knowledge, we refer to how it has been acquired and the methods by which scientists work. Doing this gives students access to a very large and important area of understanding. Learning through didactic teaching methods may enable a student to draw and label a diagram of the heart, or carry out a calculation using Ohm's Law, or describe the effect of a rise in temperature on the rate of a chemical reaction. But a good, practical scientific education can achieve much more than this. Young people who have experienced a wide range of practical work will have much more confidence in their ability to tackle new situations, to criticise and evaluate claims made for Science in the media, and – for some – to take their education further.

This chapter highlights the importance to students of carrying out practical work, whilst also recognising the difficulties that some schools face in providing opportunities for undertaking such work.

The importance of practical work in Science teaching

As mentioned above, there are many reasons for including practical work in Science lessons:

- Involvement in practical work helps students to develop the skills of a good scientist – planning investigations and selecting appropriate apparatus, careful observation and measurement, accurate recording and clear display of results, drawing logical conclusions from them and assessing their reliability.
- Carrying out practical work helps students to understand facts and concepts.
- Participation in practical work encourages active learning rather than passive learning, provided the students are required to think about the purpose of the practical activity. It gives students the confidence to think and do for themselves, rather than always relying on the teacher to spoon-feed them with knowledge.
- Practical work can make phenomena more real (see, for example, Figure 2.1).

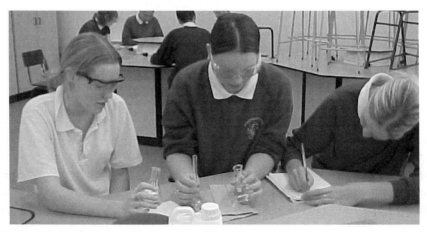

Figure 2.1: Students investigating the effect
of temperature on the rate of enzyme action

- Practical work adds variety and interest to Science lessons.
- Almost all Science examinations test practical skills in some way. Even if this is done by written assessment – for example Paper 6 in any of the IGCSE Science syllabuses – students will do better in this part of the examination if they have had direct experience of practical work.
- Practical work helps to develop cross-curricular skills such as communication, literacy, numeracy and ICT. The ability to work as part of a team is often important.

The earlier that practical work can be introduced into a student's education the better. If you are working in a school that students enter well before their IGCSE years, then it is important to ensure that they do practical work on a regular basis as soon as they start studying Science. By the time they embark on their IGCSE courses, they will be very experienced at doing practicals and will have learned the disciplines required for working in a laboratory.

Difficulties in introducing practical work into Science teaching

Although most Science teachers will agree that their Science lessons should include practical work, in many cases this does not happen. The reasons that teachers give for not doing practical work fall into three main categories:
- lack of facilities;
- time pressure;
- class size.

Lack of facilities

We don't have good laboratory facilities in my school; there is hardly any equipment and we don't have a laboratory technician.

A school that attempts to include Science in its curriculum without providing adequate laboratory facilities is not really giving optimum support for its students. These facilities do not need to be sophisticated: the main requirements are a water supply, an electrical supply and some means of heating (Bunsen or spirit burners), plus a safe area where students can work. You will also need a range of containers (preferably but not necessarily glassware) and basic measuring instruments. Obviously, it is desirable to have much more than this, but the lack of sophisticated equipment or facilities is not a reason for avoiding practical work altogether. Schools with very limited resources and facilities need to select carefully practicals that can be carried out with the minimum of equipment and in ordinary classrooms, or even outside, as fieldwork (see Figure 2.2).

Figure 2.2: Fieldwork is an option when laboratory facilities are limited

Even when a teacher has to rely on demonstrating practicals due to lack of class sets of equipment or poor laboratory facilities, students can be actively involved in the process, changing the learning style from passive to active. Ways of approaching this sort of practical work are considered in Chapter 3.

Appendix C lists appropriate equipment to use in the teaching of IGCSE Biology, Chemistry and Physics. This will be useful for a teacher wishing to extend Science resources or set up a new laboratory. *Planning for practical Science in secondary schools*, published by Cambridge International Examinations (CIE), contains more detailed information.

Many schools do not have support from laboratory technicians. Once again, although it is obviously very desirable to have such support, it is possible to do a great deal of practical work without it – and very many teachers do. It may be helpful to ask for volunteers amongst your keenest, most reliable students to contribute in a technical role – setting up trays of equipment, washing glassware and so on. If managed well, this can be very prestigious for those students. For a school that gives students badges for key roles (prefect, librarian etc.), a laboratory technician's badge would be appropriate.

Time pressure

We would never get through the course in time if we did practical work.

If this is a problem for you, then look closely at the time your school allocates for covering the course you are teaching. All of the IGCSE and O Level Science courses, for example, are intended to be taught over two full years, with between $2\frac{1}{2}$ and 3 hours a week of contact time.[1] Each syllabus has been written with the intention that practical work will be an integral part of the course, and the required breadth and depth of treatment of the subject content of the syllabus has been limited accordingly. It can be argued that if practical assessment is worth, for example, 20% of the final mark in an examination (as is the case in IGCSE sciences) then a minimum of 20% of the time should be spent on practical work.

Also, look at the depth to which you cover your subject. Inexperienced teachers often attempt to go into much more detail than is required by the syllabus. This not only takes time, but can also confuse students if difficult concepts are introduced before they are ready to deal with them. Teaching to the level stated in the syllabus and doing plenty of practical work and other activities that develop skills as well as knowledge is the best way of ensuring good examination results.

Class size

I have about 40 students in my classes. We don't have the space for them all to do practical work, and anyway I would worry about discipline if they were out of their seats and moving around.

There is no doubt that large class sizes make doing practical work very difficult. A sensible maximum is probably about 30, although the size of the room in which they are working will obviously affect this. If you do have very large classes, then consider the possibility of splitting the class for one session a week and using this session for practical work.

LOOKING BACK

- What are the main issues that prevent you from doing practical work or restrict your ability to do so?
- What could you do to overcome these problems?

---

[1] The IGCSE Coordinated Science course is an exception – this is intended to be covered in double the time that would be appropriate for one single Science course.

3 Planning the practical content of a Science course

This chapter is concerned with the apparatus, equipment and resources needed to undertake practical work effectively. It considers innovative approaches to apparatus, in terms of both using existing apparatus in alternative ways and adapting easily available, everyday items for use in Science practicals. It then considers technological developments that can benefit practical work, particularly data logging.

It is important that teachers in a department intending to increase its use of practicals to improve learning assess what equipment they have and what practicals should be run, making best use of the resources available. A good starting point would be to carry out an audit, with the aim of identifying the apparatus available in the department, appropriate practicals and any extra apparatus needed to run these. Use all the expertise available to you, involving other experienced staff and technician(s). Study your syllabus or scheme of work section by section, noting suitable practical opportunities, the equipment needed and, finally, recording what you actually have in the department. You can then add practicals that are feasible with the resources available to your scheme of work or syllabus. Most Science textbooks include experiments to draw ideas from, so also check these chapter by chapter for suitable ideas. On completion of the audit, you will have a clear picture of how to develop the practical side of the course(s) you run. Owing to limited stocks of some pieces of apparatus, or through safety considerations, some practicals will need to be in the form of demonstrations rather than whole class activities. As stated earlier, for large classes it may be necessary to run a practical with half the class while the remainder are given a written task.

Carry out an audit for one topic that you teach:

- Make a copy of your scheme of work (or syllabus) for that topic.
- Create two columns to the right of the subject content and in these identify appropriate practicals and the apparatus needed to run these. Highlight the apparatus not available in your department and consider whether you could use alternatives.
- Cross-reference the topic in a range of textbooks to get fresh ideas for practicals you have not tried.

Alternative uses of apparatus

A suitable range of standard apparatus is listed in Appendix C. The items listed have four functions:

- measurement (length, volume, mass, time);
- containment (to carry out reactions and make observations);
- manipulation of materials;
- safety.

We tend to have fixed ideas about the uses of pieces of apparatus. However, it is surprising just how versatile some can be, as illustrated below.

Measuring cylinders are traditionally used for measuring volumes of liquid accurately. More innovative applications include those outlined in Student activities 3.1 to 3.3.

Student activity 3.1

This involves the measurement of volumes of gas generated during an enzyme-controlled reaction (e.g. the breakdown of hydrogen peroxide by catalase).

Catalase is naturally present in many types of vegetable, including potatoes and carrots, and also in animal tissue such as liver. If a source of catalase is added to hydrogen peroxide, oxygen is generated. The reaction is carried out in a sealed conical flask with side arm and delivery tube, or delivery tube extending from a cork stopper. A boiling tube in place of the conical flask is also workable. The gas is collected over water in an inverted measuring cylinder, initially full of water. Readings of the gas trapped can be taken easily using the graduations on the cylinder. If the conical flask is contained in a water bath or bowl, the temperature of its contents can be controlled. The effect of temperature on enzyme rate can then be investigated.

The same arrangement can be used for investigating rates of reaction in Chemistry. This experiment is a more sophisticated version of the practical that involves counting bubbles. The problem with bubble counting is the lack of accuracy involved – bubble sizes vary. The version using a measuring cylinder is one way of improving the bubble counting experiment.

Student activity 3.2

This experiment, looking at the increase in volume of bread dough as it rises, is linked to respiration. Since respiration is controlled by enzymes, students should be made aware that they are monitoring an enzyme-controlled reaction and consider this in their planning and explanations in the conclusion.

Yeast-based dough is prepared and rolled into a sausage shape, cut to length and placed in the cylinder so that the dough occupies about a third of its height. The measuring cylinder can then be placed in a water bath or bowl containing water at a chosen temperature. Repeat at different temperatures. The effect of temperature on the rate of dough expansion can then be investigated. If you find that the dough is difficult to remove from the measuring cylinder at the end of the practical, beakers are a suitable alternative, although the graduations up the side are not as accurate: the height of the dough could be read with a ruler instead.

Student activity 3.3

In this activity, the volumes of irregular solids are measured by the difference in reading when the solid is placed into a measuring cylinder containing water. If a suitable balance is available, densities of different materials can be determined and compared, using the formula:

$$\text{density} = \frac{\text{mass}}{\text{volume}}$$

Measuring cylinders can be of glass or plastic. The plastic variety tends to be more durable but they can become more opaque with age, making accurate readings less easy. However, for a school with a limited budget, plastic measuring cylinders will probably be more economical and, with little chance of breakage, younger or less experienced students will be more confident in handling them.

For schools without a good stock of pipettes or measuring cylinders, **plastic syringes** are inexpensive, very easy to use and are available in a range of different sizes. Although **beakers** do have some graduations on the side, these are only rough guides and should not be used where accurate measuring is required. Even where no measuring instrument is available, a range of concentrations of a solution can be created by students (see Student activity 3.4).

Student activity 3.4

Start with a known concentration of the liquid. Pour some of this into a container such as a test tube. Mark the level with an indelible marker pen, or put a sticker at the base of the meniscus. Pour this liquid into a second, larger container (boiling tube, beaker or jar).

Repeat with water – fill the test tube to the same level. Add this to the liquid in the boiling tube. Its concentration is now half that of the original solution. The strategy can then be used to produce other dilutions. These are suitable for rate of reaction investigations or, if a sugar solution is prepared, the effect of solute concentration on osmosis in potato.

Cork borers are ideal for cutting cylinders of plant material. If the cylinders are cut to the same length, two variables (surface area and volume) are controlled very effectively.

Metal bottle tops make convenient containers for heating small amounts of solids. They need to be burned in a blue Bunsen flame to remove any plastic before being used for practicals.

Sand trays make satisfactory alternatives to heat mats.

Small sand bags can be used in place of newton weights.

Suggestions for experiments

There are many experiments and investigations that can be run with the minimum of apparatus. Some are listed in Tables 3.1a (Biology), 3.1b (Chemistry) and 3.1c (Physics), but this selection is by no means exhaustive. The *Science teachers' handbook* (Byers, Childs and Laine, 1994) also provides an excellent range of suggestions for alternative equipment and activities using local materials.

The availability of chemicals may be an issue. Again, there are often alternatives that allow effective practical work to be carried out. Some are suggested in the selection in Table 3.1b. Household chemicals used in the kitchen and bathroom can provide a range of pH. Aluminium foil and iron scouring pads can be used in experiments involving burning metals. Matches provide a useful source of sulphur dioxide. Indicators can be made from plants such as red cabbage, black beans and beetroot.

Table 3.1a: Experiments and investigations that can be run with the minimum of apparatus: Biology

Title	Apparatus, chemical and other materials	Brief outline
The effect of exercise on pulse rate	• stopwatches or clock with second hand	Students measure their resting pulse, then they exercise. They monitor pulse rate for at least five minutes after exercise, then repeat, keeping the exercise the same.
Comparing sensitivity of skin on different parts of the body	• rod with sliding corks • supporting pins	Start with the pins 2 cm apart. Rest pins on back of partner's hand ten times – sometimes one pin, sometimes two. Record success at stating how many pins have been felt. If seven or more out of ten, reduce the distance between pins by 0.5 cm. Stop at 0.5 cm. Then test other skin areas.
The effect of acid rain on plants	• coffee jars • petri dish lids or sheets of glass • matches • petroleum jelly • modelling clay • moss or other small plants such as cress seedlings, or aquatic plants	Use sets of four jars. Place a piece of healthy moss (or a few plant seedlings) at the bottom of each. Then add: • Jar 1 – clay only; • Jar 2 – clay with one live match; • Jar 3 – clay with two live matches; • Jar 4 – clay with three live matches. Smear the jar rims with petroleum jelly. Light the match(es). Immediately seal the jar with the petri dish/glass sheet to trap the gas (SO_2). Leave for a few days in the light. Observe changes to the moss.
Heart dissection	• boards or shallow dishes • scalpels, scissors or sharp razor blades • mounted needles with blunt tip or old pencils • hearts	Observe the intact heart first, identifying atria, ventricles, major blood vessels, coronary arteries and fat deposits. If a tap is available, try forcing water through the heart from a vein. Open the right atrium and ventricle to expose valves. Use the mounted needle or pencil to show the relationship between chambers and blood vessels. Repeat with left side, comparing thickness of ventricle walls.

Effect of light intensity on photosynthesis	• lamp • ruler • beaker or jar • Elodea or similar pond plant	Cut the end of the Elodea stem and then place it in water in the beaker. Set up the lamp a measured distance from the plant, e.g. 20 cm. Allow the plant to adjust to this light intensity. Record number of O_2 bubbles produced in a fixed time, e.g. a minute. Repeat at different distances. Plot a graph of light intensity $(1/d^2)$ against number of bubbles.
Reaction time	• rulers (30 cm) • blindfolds	Students work in pairs. One student holds the ruler above their partner's hand. When they release it, their partner has to catch it. Record the length of ruler below the partner's hand. Repeat ten times. Then try with the first student blindfolded, or with loud music playing. Compare sets of results.
Predicting the outcomes of genetic crosses	• plastic beads or dried peas • large beakers or other dry containers	Use two beakers per group. Each group starts with two sets of, e.g., 20 pairs of beads (use different colours; if using peas, colour them with felt-tipped pens) that represent the genotypes of the parents. Each bead therefore represents an allele (in sex cells). Randomly remove a single bead from each beaker and record the combination of each pair produced (this is the F1 offspring). When all the beads have been removed and paired, calculate the ratios produced. Try again with parents of different genotypes.

Table 3.1b: Experiments and investigations that can be run with the minimum of apparatus: Chemistry

Title	Apparatus, chemical and other materials	Brief outline
pH testing	• beakers and test tubes • droppers or syringes • a range of household chemicals • indicator solution	Set up the household chemicals in labelled beakers. Use one dropper per beaker. Students transfer a few drops to a test tube, add a few drops of indicator solution and record the colour produced.
Neutralisation, salt production	• evaporating basin • beaker • means of measuring liquids • heat source • hydrochloric acid and sodium hydroxide, or vinegar and sodium hydrogencarbonate	Use HCl and NaOH of the same concentration. Mix equal amounts. Test the solution produced with indicator paper to make sure neutralisation is complete. Evaporate to near dryness. Collect salt.
Heating metals in air	• bottle tops • tongs • tripod and gauze • heat source • a range of metals • beakers	Bottle caps can be held with tongs or placed on the corner of a gauze, supported on a tripod. Place a metal in the bottle cap and heat strongly. Observe any reaction.
Reactions of metals with acid	• beakers and test tubes • hydrochloric acid • range of metals (e.g. Cu, Fe, Mg, Zn, Pb, Al)	Place the metals in test tubes. Add an equal amount of acid to each. Observe any reactions. Test any gas with a burning splint.
Displacement of metals	• spotting tiles • droppers • beakers or test tubes • a range of metals and metal salts	For each salt, place a small amount in depressions in the spotting tile (one for each metal). Add a different metal to each depression. Repeat with the other salts. Observe any reactions. Use the observations to place the metals in order of reactivity.
Effect of concentration on rate of reaction	• conical flasks or beakers • means of measuring liquids • means of timing • hydrochloric acid • sodium thiosulphate • paper with cross drawn on it	Students make a range of dilutions of the sodium thiosulphate. 50 cm^3 of the highest concentration is added to 5 cm^3 of 2.0 mol/dm^3 acid in a conical flask, placed over the cross. The time for the cross to disappear is recorded. Repeat with other dilutions. Effect of light intensity.

Table 3.1c: Experiments and investigations that can be run with the minimum of apparatus: Physics

Title	Apparatus, chemical and other materials	Brief outline
Air resistance	• stopwatches • tape measure or metre stick • paper or card (for 'helicopters') and scissors	Fold strips of card to produce wings with a vertical body. Drop from a measured height. Time how long the 'helicopter' takes to reach the ground. Repeat with other helicopters with wings of different areas.
Gravity/forces	• newspaper and scissors • string • egg • Sellotape	Challenge students to design, make and, eventually, test a way of transporting an egg from, for example, a first floor window to the ground without the egg breaking. Evaluate the successful and unsuccessful designs.
Forces	• newton weights or sand bags of known mass • paper and scissors • drinking straws • Sellotape	Design, build and test a bridge made out of straws and paper to support a certain weight. The bridge must have a minimum unsupported span.
Moments	• metre sticks or sticks with equal graduations on • selection of equal weights or small sand bags • nail • clamp and stand or other means of supporting the metre stick	Support the metre stick with the nail through its centre. Hang a load from one end. Attach a different load to the other end and move it along until the beam is balanced. Record the loads and their distances from the pivot. Repeat with other loads, varying the distance of the first from the pivot.
Speed of sound	• measuring tape • stopwatches • wood blocks	Split the class into two groups and arrange them a reasonably large, measured distance apart (at least 150 metres – this should give a time of about 0.5 seconds). One group has the wood blocks; the other has the stop watch. One student is instructed to wave while another hits the blocks together. The second group records the time elapsed between observing the student waving and hearing the bang. The speed of sound can then be calculated.
Conduction in metals	• range of metal rods • heat source • nails or drawing pins • tripod or other support for rods • petroleum jelly or wax	Make sure all the rods are the same length (and, ideally, the same diameter). Attach a drawing pin to each rod using the wax or petroleum jelly. Balance the rods on a tripod. Heat the ends of the rods equally. Record the order in which the pins drop off, to compare the conductivity of the different metals.

Even in a Science department where equipment is in very short supply, demonstration experiments can be performed in such a way as to actively involve the whole class (see Student activity 3.5).

Student activity 3.5

Discuss possible strategies for the investigation with the class: planning, selecting appropriate apparatus, formulating a hypothesis, making predictions, controlling variables. One volunteer could record the main points on the board for later reference, allowing you to give the class your full attention. Then ask for a volunteer to carry out the practical. The rest of the class is likely to take a far greater interest and be more prepared to make suggestions, raise safety issues and give other advice than if the teacher was demonstrating the experiment in the traditional way. If duplicate results are to be collected, allow other volunteers to become involved. Ask others in the class to record results as they are collected. The whole class assumes ownership of the practical. For future experiments, rotate the volunteers so that, eventually, everyone has the opportunity to have hands-on experience of practical work.

Student activity 3.6 suggests an unusual way of familiarising a class with common items of laboratory glassware. This can be used in Biology when introducing the use of keys in classification.

Student activity 3.6

Split the class into groups. Provide each group with five or six items, such as a measuring cylinder, beaker, boiling tube, test tube, conical flask and jam jar (or coffee jar). Instruct them to decide on a feature that will split the items into two groups. For each of these subgroups, repeat the process until all the items have been separated. Compare the strategies used by different groups – not all will have used the same route to separate the items. Features such as graduations, pouring spout, neck and the ability to stand unsupported will be identified. Finally show the group how a key can be created, based on the objects they have classified. For example:

1 Has the item got a spout?
    If yes, go to 2. If no, go to 5.
2 Is the item tall and thin, with graduations?
    If yes = measuring cylinder. If no, go to 3.
etc.

Technological developments
Data logging in Science

Advances in technology allow for the accurate capture and processing of data without practicals becoming time-consuming and repetitious. Teachers finding it difficult to devote the time for practical work will obviously benefit from the introduction of this type of equipment, leaving time to concentrate on experimental planning, concluding and evaluation. Where possible, students should have the opportunity to use data logging equipment and, through this, will develop an appreciation of its benefits in scientific research. However, there are substantial drawbacks to data logging equipment: it is very expensive, difficult to use and not always reliable. Talk to colleagues in other schools to see what they have found successful and cost effective before spending a lot of money on this sort of equipment.

Data logging equipment usually consists of three sets of components:
- sensors, to detect stimuli;
- a data logging device to capture and store the data;
- software to process the data on computer.

The data logger usually runs on batteries, so data can be collected beyond the usual laboratory situation. Where electricity supplies are not constant, there are obvious advantages to apparatus that runs on batteries, although the cost of replacing these can be limiting.

Examples of data logging are in monitoring:
- variation in abiotic factors in a pond over 24 hours – air temperature, water temperature, pH (to consider carbon dioxide changes), oxygen concentration, light sensors;
- a neutralisation reaction such as the titration of sodium hydroxide with hydrochloric acid – pH and temperature sensors;
- rate of reaction by logging the loss in mass of reactants due to gas production – digital top pan balance;
- the movement of a person with time to generate a distance–time graph – distance sensor;
- the acceleration of a dropped object – light gates;
- the current in, and voltage across, an electrical component to generate the component's current–voltage (I–V) characteristic – current sensor and potential difference (PD) sensor.

If the data logger is connected to a computer, data can be processed during the course of the investigation so that students can observe the process and watch a trend develop (through graph plotting etc.). Some sensors such as temperature sensors can be used in isolation because they have their own display. These make very accurate alternatives to standard thermometers, giving temperature readings to perhaps 0.1 °C.

The Science Enhancement Programme (SEP) is a Gatsby-funded organisation that provides practical kits and web-based resources. They also supply a very cheap and easy-to-use datalogger called *ibutton*, which measures temperature (see Appendix A).

Departments without data logging systems can still teach about their use through computer simulations. There are many inexpensive software packages, available through educational software companies, that can be run as demonstrations or networked for whole class use. There are far too many to list here, but here are a few I have found to be relatively inexpensive and successful:

- *Alchemy?* is a double CD-ROM set that contains video clips of various industrial processes along with flowcharts, questions and web links.
- *ASE Science Year resources* comprises five CD-ROMs produced by the Association for Science Education. They contain a great range of activities to enliven Science lessons. For example, the program 'Flesh eaters' is a very original way of teaching about enzymes.
- *Chemistry set 2000* has video clips of hundreds of experiments, a database of information about Chemistry and photographs of minerals, details of famous chemists etc. It is extremely comprehensive and contains material that would also serve students beyond IGCSE level.
- *Crocodile clips* (for Chemistry and Physics). These allow students to design and simulate experiments that may be too dangerous or too expensive to run in the laboratory and to design and test electrical circuits.
- *PRI – ideas and evidence* is a pack of innovative student activities about topics often missing from traditional textbooks. Each unit is in the form of downloadable worksheets, supported by teacher guides. I have tried out many of these and found them to be extremely original and useful.
- *RSC electronic data book* contains a comprehensive database of elements and compounds, interactive programs and a periodic table.
- *Understanding electricity: sources of energy* provides information about renewable and non-renewable energy, transmission and distribution of electricity, pollution issues and general principles of power generation.

Details of the publishers of these CD-ROMs can be found in Appendix A.

Other items that incorporate the latest technology include digital cameras, flexi cams and digital microscopes.

Digital cameras

These are easy to use and can be employed to:

- keep a record of children working (a great way of producing interesting wall displays);
- photograph equipment involved in a practical;
- record observations (arrangement of teeth, external structure of the eye etc.);
- provide images that can be incorporated into worksheets or used in projects by students.

Various formats are available. Some have memory cards that can be removed and placed into the computer. Others can be connected to the computer by a lead to download saved images. A third type stores the images on a 3.5-inch computer floppy disk. I have found this type to be particularly useful in a classroom situation because after my students have taken the images they require, they can take their floppy disk away, leaving me in control of the camera. I can store up to 40 images on a single disk when using the standard format. The battery lasts for about 2 hours. A digital camera is one of the best pieces of modern technology I have bought for my laboratory. Students find it very straightforward to use and they include the images to produce high-quality work. Most of my classroom wall displays use images taken with a digital camera. I print out the images on ordinary printer paper and then laminate them. This gives the glossy finish of a traditional photograph and increases the life of the image. A laminator costs less than, for example, an overhead projector. Plastic pouches for laminating work cost about the same as acetates for overhead projectors.

Flexi cams

A flexi cam is a camera on a flexible stand linked to a video system. It can also be connected to a microscope to produce images on the TV screen and its images can also be stored on video tape. In addition, it can be linked to a computer. In Biology, flexi cams are ideal for running a plenary session after a practical making and observing microscope slides. I highlight details of slides to the whole class. The teacher can even label relevant features on the television screen using a whiteboard marker pen. Using this approach, you can ensure that all members of the class have seen the features you wanted them to see. In Physics, small details such as the needle of a voltmeter could be enlarged to enable a large class to view the progress of an experiment on a television screen. The quality of the images produced by a video microscope is excellent, making it ideal for whole class demonstrations.

An innovative use of a flexi cam or digital video camera is to film the progress of an investigation, such as the rate at which pieces of paper (e.g. in the form of a ball or as a flat sheet) fall. When the film clip is played back, the paper can be observed in slow motion and it is possible to measure its rate of descent.

A digital microscope is an inexpensive alternative to a flexi cam attached to a microscope. It is connected to a computer and the images produced can be printed out, stored or incorporated into documents. One slight drawback is a time lag between moving the slide around the field of view (or adjusting the focus) and the new image appearing on the computer screen.

PC projectors

A PC projector allows you to project images from a computer onto a screen or whiteboard to produce a much bigger picture than that of a monitor. It is therefore ideal for whole class work. You can make demonstrations in Microsoft PowerPoint on specific topics using illustrations imported from CD-ROMs or the Internet, or those you have taken with a digital camera, or scanned in. You can demonstrate any computer programs you intend your students to use. However, PC projectors have two drawbacks: they are very expensive to buy and the bulbs they use can be very expensive to replace. Do check on the cost of replacement bulbs when considering this type of equipment.

LOOKING BACK

This chapter considered possible approaches to increasing the practical content of a science course, making the best use of the resources available.

- Have you recently carried out an audit of your equipment? If not, use the guidelines at the start of the chapter to help you with your audit.
- Do your practicals make the best use of your equipment? If not, how could you adapt your practicals or demonstrations to do so?
- How can you involve your students in your demonstrations?

4 Practical skills

The majority of Science syllabuses state a range of practical skills that will be tested. These are usually listed as 'assessment objectives'. Although there may be apparent differences between the skills required by different syllabuses, in fact they are all extremely similar. The skills that students should learn, and that will be assessed, include:

- planning investigations;
- following instructions and working safely with apparatus and reagents;
- making observations and measurements;
- recording observations and measurements;
- handling data;
- drawing conclusions;
- evaluating the experiment.

Planning investigations

This skill in many ways underpins all the others. Students should be helped to develop the confidence to state a clear question to be answered, or a hypothesis to be tested, and then outline a simple method to investigate this. This, in the end, is what being a scientist is all about.

Following instructions and working safely with apparatus and reagents

This is the most basic of the practical skills, and one which all Science students should learn as early as possible. It is also a cross-curricular skill (essential in other subjects such as Technology) – and very much a life skill, valuable far beyond the confines of the Science laboratory. Students should also learn how to handle and use simple apparatus, for instance building an electrical circuit or assembling a simple potometer.

Making observations and measurements

Students need to learn how to observe carefully and methodically – while we do this as second nature, it is not something that most students do automatically. They need guidance and practice. They should have opportunities to observe events (e.g. what happens when magnesium is added to hydrochloric acid) and structures (e.g. the detailed structure of a leaf).

The ability to make detailed and accurate measurements is essential for any scientist. Students should have repeated opportunities to use appropriate instruments to measure time, length, mass, volume and temperature in addition to other quantities specific to particular syllabuses.

Students should also be aware that the collection of data can become very tedious and mundane! Access to data logging equipment will show them how technology can be used to reduce the 'boredom factor' in the investigative process without diminishing the accuracy of the measurements collected.

Recording observations and measurements

This involves putting the results of observation or measurement onto paper or into a computer in a way that others can quickly and easily understand. It may involve recording numerical data in a table, writing descriptions or drawing diagrams.

Handling data

Raw results often need processing or displaying. Students should be able to carry out simple calculations (e.g. a percentage change in length in an osmosis investigation) and to display results as graphs.

Drawing conclusions

Students should be given help to interpret data, including anomalous results. They should be able to see what their results mean, and to write a brief and precise conclusion that can be drawn from them. This is often far easier to do if the experiment has a clear aim or is testing a particular hypothesis.

Evaluating the experiment

This is a relatively high-level skill, and one that often differentiates between the good scientist and the very good. Students should learn to look critically at the experiment they have carried out, decide how reliable their results are, and suggest further work to improve accuracy and reliability.

Students will not acquire these skills unless you teach them! The remaining chapters in this book consider how you can help your students to acquire these skills during the Science course that you are teaching.

- Search through a copy of the Science syllabuses you follow and find the list of practical skills that will be tested. They will probably be under the heading 'assessment objectives'.
- Compare these with the skills identified in this chapter to see if there are any substantial differences.

There are a number of good textbooks available to provide you with support in helping your students to develop investigative skills, for example Goldsworthy, Watson and Wood-Robinson (2000), which consists of two volumes: *Developing understanding* and *Getting to grips with graphs.*

LOOKING BACK

- ◆ What are the practical skills in your syllabus?
- ◆ How do you ensure that you cover all of them?

5 Planning investigations

Although planning is the first stage of an investigation, many syllabuses put this experimental skill last. This is hardly surprising when you start to consider what it involves. Students need to be quite experienced in the other experimental skills before they can be expected to design their own investigations. They need to be familiar with a range of equipment and select the apparatus appropriate to the task, state an aim, make predictions and design their own method – into which the control of variables (fair testing), safety, accuracy and reliability all need to be built.

A good starting point for the students would be for them to experience carrying out investigations that have been planned for them. They will then become familiar with the standard strategy a scientist uses when investigating. Students need practice at describing experiments in their own words. This process tends to be more time-consuming than copying a method off the board or from a textbook, but will make the student more aware of the way experiments are constructed.

The topic under investigation needs to be familiar to the student – a good time to plan an investigation would therefore be at the end of a topic. Students are then far more likely to understand what they are aiming to find out.

The planning stage does not necessarily have to take place in a Science laboratory – it could take place in an ordinary classroom or in a computer room.

Use of checklists

I use checklists with all my students – even the most academic are liable to miss crucial parts out of a plan. The checklist identifies all the parts that should be present in a completed plan and it is for the student's own use. The teacher can then concentrate on assessing the quality of the content, rather than identifying the parts that are missing from it. Another way of increasing the students' awareness of what should be in a plan (and at the same time reducing your workload) is to get them to assess each other's plans. The checklist shown in Worksheet 1 (Appendix D) contains one set of tick boxes. This is for the student's own use. I sometimes include a second, for another student (or the teacher) to double-check the content. A further way of ensuring that the checklist is used properly is to number each item on the list. As students tick that each of the criteria are present, they have to write the number of that item at the appropriate place in their plan, to demonstrate where the criterion has been met.

Worksheet 1 is one I use in a British school, and is applicable to any of the sciences. You may choose to modify it to satisfy the requirements of the syllabus you teach.

I begin the planning process with a class by stating the problem and by handing out and explaining the planning checklist. I also have a range of apparatus on my teacher's bench to prompt students to start thinking about what they will need. I discuss the importance of a fair test and how to control variables. Many students get confused between how to obtain *reliable* results (through planning to collect repeat sets of data and calculating averages) and how to achieve *accurate* results (by selecting the most appropriate apparatus to measure with), so I stress the difference between the two terms.

A paragraph of background material is written by the students individually in the computer room to enable them to draw together the knowledge they already have so that they can become more familiar with the problem they have to solve. Depending on the topic, I may issue a list of relevant key words that students can use to support them as they write their plan. A topic such as osmosis involves quite a large and difficult vocabulary and a key word list definitely helps. For example, a key word list for an osmosis investigation would include:

cell	cell sap	cell wall
concentration	cytoplasm	diffusion
flaccid	membrane	molarity
plasmolysed	turgid	vacuole
water	water potential	

I set a deadline for the plan to be completed; otherwise, this part of the investigation tends to take far too long. Those who do not finish have to make up time during a lunch break (still supervised, so that I can guarantee it is the student's own work). Throughout the process, I emphasise the value of the work the students are producing as it may contribute significantly towards the practical assessment mark, representing 20% of the total exam mark. However, I also explain – to those who are over-anxious about under-achieving on their first attempt – that there will be other opportunities to plan an investigation.

Key features of checklists

Safety

Including safety in the checklist means that students have to carry out a simple risk assessment to identify possible dangers in their plan and then minimise them. This is good practice, whether in school or the workplace.

Predicting

Making a prediction and explaining it encourages students to draw on their knowledge and understanding and will make the writing of a conclusion more straightforward later. It is important to avoid guessing. You should provide enough background to help students make a valid prediction.

I develop the predicting skills of my students at every opportunity, i.e. whenever we do a practical, whether it be a demonstration or a whole class activity. In this way, predicting becomes automatic for them. For example, when demonstrating the fountain experiment in Chemistry (see Figure 5.1), I start with the apparatus disassembled, discuss the role of each part and consider the properties of ammonia. All this is done in a question-and-answer session with the students around my teaching bench. I do not feed them with information – I encourage them to tell me what they know. This makes them learn actively and builds up a picture leading to the formation of a feasible prediction. The sorts of questions I would ask are:

- What is the nature of ammonia – acid, alkali or neutral?
- How can you prove that it is an alkali/a strong alkali?
- What colour will the universal indicator paper turn if it is alkaline?
- What pH number would you expect ammonia to be?
- Ammonia has an attraction for (loves) water. What do you expect to happen when I invert the flask and put the tubing into the trough of water?

Figure 5.1: The fountain experiment being demonstrated

Praise is very important to encourage those who volunteer answers. Do not criticise a wrong answer, but work through it to explain why the answer is wrong. Do not have the same student answering every question – others will switch off and stop volunteering. Also, try to keep a balance of who gives answers in a mixed sex group (do not, for example, let the boys dominate the session). I recently observed a very experienced male colleague teaching a Chemistry lesson. The girls all chose to sit at one side of the laboratory, the boys on the other side. The teacher led a very productive question-and-answer session, but fired all the questions at the boys, completely ignoring the girls – who were also putting their hands up. When discussing this with the teacher after the lesson, he was totally unaware that he had effectively prevented the girls from participating!

I do not comment on the prediction(s) at this stage – I accept all suggestions at face value. After all, the whole point of the demonstration is to see what will happen – and confirm or disprove the prediction. If something is raised that suggests safety could be an issue, such as 'The ammonia will be drawn out of the flask' or 'The flask will smash', I discuss that point and what safety precautions we should use (all wear safety goggles, use a safety screen, move the class further away from the apparatus etc.).

To ensure the whole class is involved, if more than one prediction has been put forward I get the whole class to vote on which they think will happen. Every member of the class has to make a decision. When the demonstration is carried out, students will be fascinated to watch what happens to see if the prediction they supported is right. With a lower ability class, I might award a small prize to the person who suggested the correct prediction. This strategy encourages more students to volunteer predictions in future lessons.

With the fountain experiment, two or three predictions are likely to come out of the discussion:

- Water from the trough will be drawn up the tubing into the flask. The universal indicator solution will turn from green to blue as it mixes with the ammonia. The water will spray into the flask (the name 'fountain experiment' is a bit of a clue!).
- Ammonia from the flask will be attracted to the water in the trough. As the ammonia goes into the trough, the universal indicator solution will turn from green to blue as the ammonia dissolves in the water.
- Nothing will happen – your experiments never work! (There is always at least one sceptic in the class!)

I also encourage students to plan how they will handle the data they collect – what form their table of results will take, what calculations will be needed and whether a graph will be appropriate. This makes them even better prepared to carry out their investigation.

Providing extra support

You will notice that in the planning checklist I have used a number of subheadings. This is to help students put together their plans in a logical sequence. Starting with a blank piece of paper on which to write a plan is a daunting prospect. Providing a simple structure makes the task more approachable. Even so, less able students in particular still have great difficulty putting together a plan. One method of extra support is by providing a writing frame. Worksheet 2 shows an example of a writing frame for a Chemistry assessment, while Worksheet 3 is an example of a writing frame with a Physics context (see Appendix D for worksheets). If I use a writing frame with a group of students, I limit the top mark they could achieve, but this is realistic given the ability of the group completing it.

Some students are not good at writing prose, but have good artistic skills. They could be encouraged to draw a series of diagrams or write a flowchart to outline their plan.

Another aid to planning is the use of a variable table. Students first identify the key variables relevant to their investigation. Having brainstormed all the things that could be changed in their investigation, they then write the variable they want to find out about (the *outcome* or *dependent variable*) as the heading of the last column in an otherwise blank table. All the other variables that might affect the outcome are used as headings for the other columns. They then choose one of these *independent variables* and select different values for it. The remaining columns represent control variables: the students will need to keep these factors the same throughout the investigation. During this activity, the teacher is able to visit each group and talk to them about their thinking before allowing them to continue the investigation.

Examples of investigations

Examples of investigations that can be planned and carried out successfully by students include:

- the effect of exercise on pulse rate;
- the effect of sugar concentration on osmosis in potato (see Chapter 8);
- the effect of temperature on enzyme activity;
- the effect of light intensity on photosynthetic rate in a pond plant;
- the conditions preferred by woodlice (or another suitable invertebrate);
- the effect of size of a peanut on the amount of energy it releases when burned;

- the effect of temperature on the rate of reaction between zinc and hydrochloric acid;
- the effect of varying sodium thiosulphate concentration on the rate of reaction with hydrochloric acid;
- the effect that varying particle size of calcium carbonate has on its reaction with hydrochloric acid;
- the effect of the length (or, harder, cross-sectional area) of a wire on its resistance;
- the effect of the current or number of wire coils in an electromagnet on its strength;
- the effect of turns ratio on the output voltage of a transformer;
- the effect of the force applied to a beam on its deflection.

The Pupil Researcher Initiative (PRI) website (see Appendix A) also provides pupil briefs for investigations, with secondary sources and background reading in new real life contexts.

Student activity 5.1

Photocopy a student's plan of an investigation, making sure it is about a topic your class is studying or is familiar with. Erase the student's name to avoid any embarrassment. Give each member of the class a copy of the plan and the planning checklist (Worksheet 1, Appendix D), with each criterion numbered. Ask the class to annotate the plan (identifying where criteria have been met) and also ticking these on the planning sheet. They should count how many ticks have been achieved out of the possible total to give an impression of the quality of the plan. Afterwards, compare scores given to see if there is a consensus within the class and discuss which criteria have not been met. This will help your students to become more familiar with the features of a good plan.

LOOKING BACK

Planning an investigation can involve the student selecting appropriate equipment, stating an aim, making a prediction and designing a method in which a number of factors have to be taken into account.
- How do you help your students to ensure that they have covered everything in their planning?
- Is there any other support they might find useful?

6 Following instructions and working safely

Of all the practical skills that students should acquire during their Science course, these are the most basic and essential. Every student, no matter what their ability, should be able to reach a high standard in following a set of instructions and working safely in the laboratory. It should be noted that students need to be able not only to follow a set of instructions, but also to understand the reason for each stage.

Safety, familiarisation with equipment and basic laboratory rules should therefore be included in any scheme of work. Numerous studies have shown that the laboratory is actually one of the safest places in the school. Awareness, by you and your students, of potential risks can ensure that they are minimised. Consider making the assessment of practical skills an integral part of their practical work. If students are aware that they are being marked on their performance during practicals, they will take this more seriously and take a more active part in them.

Teacher activity 6.1

If you are entering your students for a practical examination, refer to your syllabus for details of the exercises they are likely to be required to carry out. The syllabus will be specific about what apparatus they will need to be familiar with and be required to use proficiently.

Apparatus

Following instructions is inevitably going to involve the use of a range of basic laboratory equipment. Some of this is common to all of the sciences while some is more specific. The range of apparatus with which students should be familiar will vary to some extent from one syllabus to another. Students need to be familiar with the names of the commonest items they use, some of which are shown in Worksheet 4 (Appendix D). You could devise a simple practical to test or improve familiarity with these items (see Student activity 6.1).

Put students into groups, providing each group with a tray of all the items shown in Worksheet 4 and a set of name cards from Worksheet 5 (see Appendix D for both worksheets). If you are unable to display all the items, you could use Worksheet 4 as picture cards. The students have to place the correct name card next to each item.

The cards can be laminated, or covered with sticky backed plastic, to increase their shelf life. I keep the sets separate in envelopes, numbering the reverse of all cards in each set in case they become mixed up.

You will find more information on using apparatus for making measurements in Chapter 7.

Types of instruction

At the beginning of their Science course, students will need very precise instructions to help them to carry out practical work safely and effectively. As they gain more experience, you should begin to leave at least some of the detailed decision-making up to them, as this encourages them to think about what they are doing. Eventually they will have built up enough experience and confidence to be able to plan their own experiment and carry it out. (Details of the planning process have already been covered in Chapter 5.)

There are several ways by which you can present instructions, including:

- verbal instructions and demonstrations;
- a worksheet.

Verbal instructions

A very good way of introducing a new technique is to demonstrate what to do. It is also helpful to students whose reading skills in English are not strong. Some suggestions about demonstrations have been outlined in Chapter 2. Before carrying out a demonstration, it is important that you have all the students in a position where they can see what is going on and can be actively involved in the process. My laboratory is based on an octagonal bench system, which is excellent for whole class practicals since all students have space around them, and access to all main resources (electricity, gas and water) is nearby (see Figure 6.1).

Figure 6.1:
Students working
in a laboratory
with octagonal
benches

However, those on the far benches are not close enough to see any detail when I am demonstrating from my teacher's desk. I therefore bring them, with their chairs, to sit in an arc around my desk during a demonstration. This means they can see what I am showing them, they are less likely to get distracted (and I am more likely to notice if they do) and I do not need to shout to the corners of the laboratory. The whole arrangement makes for a more intimate and relaxed atmosphere. Of course, your arrangements will depend on the layout of your laboratory. Some laboratories have moveable benches. Do take the effort to arrange these to suit your teaching style. In a laboratory with rows of fixed benches with the teacher's bench facing them, it may be necessary to have one line of students sitting on stools in front of the teacher's bench, then a line of students sitting behind the first bench and students sitting on the second bench, with any overflow standing behind them. The main point is that all students are close enough to see what is being demonstrated and no one has their view blocked.

If you are demonstrating a method that you then want the students to repeat afterwards, avoid showing them the result – leave something for them to discover for themselves (otherwise you may get the attitude 'What's the point of doing this, the teacher has already shown us what happens.'). While carrying out the demonstration, make sure the students do not just sit passively – involve them all the time with challenging questions about the procedure, safety and predictions. Get the students to tell you what to do or what not to do, and why. Consider asking individual students to do some of the tasks you are showing them. As suggested in Chapter 3, ask a student to record each stage of the procedure on the board for reference later and to act as a summary of the process you are demonstrating.

Using a worksheet

Worksheets are a good way of giving instructions, because students can refer to the worksheet whenever they are unsure of what to do next. A worksheet with a detailed method on it can be kept by students (see, for example, Worksheet 6, Appendix D), so that they do not have to waste time copying out the method into their workbook – they can concentrate on the results and what they mean.

Where your students' reading skills are not strong, it may be a good strategy to use worksheets that make extensive use of diagrams and the minimum use of words. In any event, make sure the words used are appropriate to the average reading age of the students and do not create an obstacle to the process of following the instructions. An example is given in Worksheet 7 (Appendix D).

When teaching students how to build electrical circuits, it can be helpful to them if you leave a fully set-up, working circuit, which they can look at and compare with their own. This can avoid the flurry of 'Mine doesn't work', due to analogue meters being connected the wrong way round or digital meters being incorrectly set up. If students can identify and correct their own mistakes, those mistakes are less likely to be repeated next time.

Examples of similar worksheets are shown the booklet, *IGCSE Science – assessment of practical skills* (UCLES, 2000).

Encouraging self-reliance

One of the downsides of using worksheets with detailed instructions is that students can become very passive in their use of them. They simply follow them through like a cookery recipe, with no thought about what they are doing or why they are doing it. They then find it difficult to answer examination questions that require them to explain the reasons for parts of a process. For example, a question might ask them:

- to suggest a technique to use in an unfamiliar situation;
- how a technique might be modified in particular circumstances;
- why a particular step is carried out.

Without an understanding of their practical work, they will not be able to answer such questions.

Worksheet 7 has spaces where students are required to give reasons for some of the stages involved. This makes them think about what they are doing and why they are doing it.

To get the maximum benefit from the practical work that they do, students should be encouraged to become actively involved in thinking about the sequence of activities that is specified on the worksheet they use. There are various methods you can use.

Strategies to encourage thinking

Involve the students in thinking through the method you are going to use. Do this by questioning and discussion. You might sometimes integrate this approach with a demonstration. Table 6.1 shows how you might go about this. It is unlikely that you will always have time to do this, but if you can do it on at least some occasions that will help the learning process.

Table 6.1: A strategy for building an understanding of how to test a leaf for starch

Prior knowledge – how to test for starch using iodine solution
                 – the structure of a leaf – waxy cuticle, cell layers, starch inside cells

1 Show students a plant or leafy shoot – explain that they are going to find out if there is starch in the leaf. Ask them 'What do you use to test for starch?' 'What happens if there is starch present?' 'What happens if there is no starch present?'

2 Remove a leaf from the plant and place it on a tile. Drop some iodine solution onto it. Show the students what has happened (the iodine will simply sit on the surface of the leaf and the leaf will not change colour.

3 Ask them to suggest why the iodine solution has not changed colour. Someone may suggest that there is no starch in the leaf. This is a sensible suggestion, so accept it as a possibility.

4 Using an OHT, blackboard or whiteboard, show an outline of a transverse section through a leaf – include the mesophyll cells, the epidermis and the waxy cuticle. Ask the students where the starch would be if there were any. Try to draw out the answer that the starch is inside the cells, inside the mesophyll (palisade or spongy) layers.

5 Ask them what might be stopping the iodine from getting to the starch. Draw out the answer that the waxy cuticle is waterproof, so iodine solution (which contains water) cannot pass through it. They should also be able to tell you that the cell surface membranes control what goes in and out of cells – so they are stopping the iodine solution getting into the cells where the starch is.

6 Summarise the problem – it is necessary to break down the waxy cuticle and the cell membranes to allow the iodine to get to any starch. Explain that boiling the leaf will achieve this.

7 Place a leaf into boiling water for a few minutes. Take it out, and add the iodine solution again. Point out that the green colour makes it difficult to be sure of any colour changes. Explain that you can remove the chlorophyll using hot alcohol, because chlorophyll is soluble in alcohol.

8 Now demonstrate the whole sequence. At the appropriate point, ask the students 'Why am I heating the alcohol indirectly rather than with a flame?' Students should be aware that alcohol is flammable, so a fire could start.

Sentence completion cards

Use sets of sentence completion cards to test students' knowledge of the sequence of stages in an experiment and their understanding of the reason for doing each stage. See Student activity 6.2 and Worksheet 8 (Appendix D) for an example.

Student activity 6.2

I cut up the cards (laminating them gives them a longer life) and place them in envelopes. I give one envelope to each group of two or three students, so you may need ten or twelve envelopes per class. I give each set of cards a number. Each individual card in each set is then given that number (written on the back), in case sets get muddled up during use. I point out that each pair of cards makes a sentence, so half the cards begin with a capital letter (the start of the sentence), while the other half end with a full stop. Students then arrange the cards on the table, physically rearranging them until the sentences and the sequence are correct. I then confirm their arrangement before they copy the statements into their exercise book.

Incomplete worksheets

Prepare and use worksheets that deliberately omit some steps or details, so that students have to think and make a decision at some point. (Note that if you are assessing 'Following instructions' for any of the IGCSE sciences students cannot be awarded a maximum mark unless they do this.)

Planning discussions

Present a question or hypothesis to the class, and ask them, in groups, to discuss how they might go about investigating this. You will find much more about this in Chapter 5.

Working safely

There is nothing more important when practical work is being carried out than working safely. You and your students need to take safety very seriously. However, do remember that thousands of students all over the world are carrying out practical work in laboratories every day and accidents are rare.

The design and layout of your laboratory should acknowledge the importance of safety. If possible, try to have separate areas for sitting and writing, and for carrying out practical work. It is also very important that you can always see what is going on – try not to have areas where students are working behind high desk fronts, preventing you from seeing them. If you are lucky enough to be involved in the design of a new laboratory, then research your options thoroughly. The CIE booklet *Planning for practical Science in secondary schools* provides useful guidance. Any laboratory design has its drawbacks. It is worth visiting other schools with a range of layouts and discussing these layouts with the teachers who use them. You will then be in a better position to judge what will suit you best and you will be aware of potential problems and plan to overcome them in your day-to-day teaching. I really like my suite of laboratories with their octagonal benching, but I know of other teachers who have the opposite opinion for that sort of laboratory plan!

In most schools, students learn from the start that there are certain things that you never do in a laboratory. Each school has its own set of rules, but these will usually include the points shown in Worksheet 9 (Appendix D). As well as displaying these in a prominent place in every Science laboratory in my school, I instruct all students to paste a copy into the front of their Science exercise books to which they can refer.

Providing students with a range of solutions for an investigation is fine if you have good technical support to produce these, or if you have experience in making them yourself. If you need assistance or advice, it is worth trying websites of organisations such as CLEAPSS (www.cleapss.org.uk), which provides advice about handling chemicals and safety. In Britain, schools pay for the service. An international section may be available to support your school's Science department.

Teacher activity 6.2

Plan an introductory lesson for a new class with no experience of practical work. The lesson may include:

- discussing laboratory rules, possibly using Worksheet 9 (Appendix D);
- identifying safety features of the laboratory;
- discussing strategies to avoid accidents (some textbooks have cartoon pictures of potential hazards in a laboratory that form the basis for a useful activity);
- considering hazard symbols used in Science. These can be found in most textbooks and also on the Internet.

7 Making observations and measurements

These skills are fundamental to almost any practical work, and many investigations and experiments require the use of both.

Making observations

One of the most important practical skills is the ability to make relevant, detailed and accurate observations. As experienced scientists, it is very easy for us to take this skill for granted, but students do not automatically do it well – they need training through practical work.

Characteristics of observations

Observational skills involve noting the details of something, perhaps in order to make comparisons to distinguish one feature or result from others. Tables 7.1a (Biology), 7.1b (Chemistry) and 7.1c (Physics) contain some examples of observations that may be made in Science lessons.

When observing changes, it is very important for students to state the initial appearance as well as the final appearance.

Observations involving colours can be very difficult to make accurately, since we have to make a judgement on these. It is made easier when we are comparing the colour with a range on a colour chart (such as with pH measurements). Bear in mind that colour blindness is a surprisingly common condition, so do not be shocked when a student writes down colours that are inappropriate! Colour blindness is more common in males than in females: about 2% of males are red colour-blind, 6% of males are green colour-blind. However, only 0.4% of females show any sign of colour blindness (source: Green, Stout, Taylor and Soper, 1997, *Biological Science 1 & 2*).

Table 7.1a: Opportunities for making observations: Biology

Colour changes in food tests
These may be a single colour change, such as in the Biuret test for protein – changing from a colourless solution or suspension to the formation of a purple colour or a violet halo when protein is present.

The reducing sugar test can produce a range of colours, changing from turquoise, to pale green, yellow, mustard and, finally, red.

Features used in the classification of organisms
Most syllabuses state that these only need to be external features. Students need to decide on which details are useful as comparisons – these need to be chosen first before making the observations. For vertebrates these include details about the skin (fur, feathers, hair, scales, moist skin), appendages (arms, legs, wings, fins, flippers), shape of head and features on it (noting position of eyes, presence and shape of ears, features associated with the mouth such as teeth and beak), tail and so on.

Comparing varieties of apples
This involves noting size, colour, smell, texture, taste (see Chapter 8 for further details).

Characteristics of living things
The observations are used to distinguish between living organisms and non-living objects.

Cell structure
Here the observations may be in the form of labelled or annotated drawings.

Reaction of roots or shoots to gravity or light
These observations may be made over a period of a few days.

Comparing the structural adaptations of wind-pollinated and insect-pollinated flowers
Again, labelled or annotated drawings may be an integral part of making these observations.

Table 7.1b: Opportunities for making observations: Chemistry

Many observations are made in Chemistry because of the plethora of physical and chemical changes that are involved.

Testing the conductivity of substances
Each substance (from a range of metals and non-metals, various liquids and molten lead bromide) is put into a simple circuit containing a battery and bulb. The bulb lights if the material conducts electricity. The solids can be connected into the circuit using crocodile clips, the liquids by dipping graphite rods into them. Note that lead bromide will produce choking brown bromine vapour, so use small amounts, with plenty of ventilation, or demonstrate the reaction in a fume cupboard.

Comparing the reactivity of a range of metals (e.g. Fe, Mg, Cu, Pb, Al, Zn) in hydrochloric acid
The amount of bubbling can be used to compare reactivity. Students can also note heat generation. Aluminium gives an unexpected result for students who are aware of the reactivity series, due to a fine layer of aluminium oxide on the surface that protects it. Rubbing the surface of the metal with fine sand paper or emery cloth can make a difference.

Displacement of metals from their salts
Here, a reaction is identified by colour changes in the solution and on the surface of the metal. This is a good practical for putting metals in order of their reactivity.

Burning metals or their salts in air
The colour of the flame is noted and used as a distinguishing feature to identify unknowns.

Testing the strength of acids and alkalis using pH paper or solution
Colours produced are noted. These can then be converted to pH values using a colour chart.

Comparing the solubility of substances
This can be approached in a number of ways:
- studying the effect of the temperature of a solvent on the solubility of a single solute (e.g. water and sugar);
- comparing the solubility of different solutes;
- comparing different solvents.

In each of these experiments the student notes whether the substance has dissolved completely by observing if there is any undissolved material remaining in the beaker.

The fountain experiment (also referred to in Chapter 5)
This demonstrates the solubility of a gas (either ammonia or hydrogen chloride). With ammonia, I place a small amount of concentrated ammonium hydroxide solution into a round bottomed flask. The flask is stoppered, with a thin glass delivery tube running from it. I warm the flask to encourage the gas to evaporate, forcing air out of the tube. Once the flask is fully saturated with gas, the ammonia begins to come out of the tube – and can be tested using damp blue litmus paper. The flask is then clamped upside down, with the end of the delivery tube submerged in a trough of water, containing universal indicator solution. The solution is drawn up the tube and as it enters the flask it sprays out (hence the name 'fountain experiment'), changing colour as the ammonia dissolves in it. Students can observe the initial colour of the solution in the trough, its movement against gravity up the tube, the way it sprays into the flask and the colour change of the solution as it meets the ammonia.

Table 7.1c: Opportunities for making observations: Physics

Studying the polarity of magnets
Observations can be made about which combinations of poles attract or repel.

Field lines around a magnet
If a magnet is placed under a sheet of white paper and iron filings are shaken onto the paper, field lines appear that can be observed and drawn.

Bulbs in series and parallel
When a number of bulbs are placed in a series circuit their brightness can be observed. The same number of bulbs can then be tested in parallel and their brightness compared with the previous situation. The number of bulbs can then be varied in each circuit.

The appearance of planets
These can be observed and compared, using photographs in textbooks or images downloaded from the Internet.

Phases of the moon
Students can make observations over 27 days (the time for one orbit around the earth) on a nightly basis, as long as the sky is clear enough!

Dynamo
Observe the effect of increasing the speed at which a dynamo is turned on the brightness of a bulb attached to it. A similar exercise could be carried out using a solar panel attached to a propeller, changing the intensity of the light falling on the panel and noting its effect on the rate at which the propeller turns.

Observational drawings

The drawings most commonly undertaken by students at this level are those of cells and tissues, sometimes to show their relationships with each other – as in a transverse section of a leaf. Often, students will be reluctant to attempt drawing from observation: 'I'm not an artist, I can't draw' is a common comment I hear. The satisfaction of producing a good drawing for the first time, praised by the teacher, soon enables the student to get over this hurdle. Usual mistakes made by inexperienced students include making the drawing too small, making the proportions incorrect, having sketchy lines that represent membranes or cell walls and using a pencil that is blunt or too hard or too soft. Elaborately shaded drawings are unnecessary. Students are also tempted to draw groups of cells even when they have been instructed to draw a single cell.

It is good practice to demonstrate how to approach a cell drawing before allowing your students to attempt it. To avoid them copying my drawing, I demonstrate with a different cell, using a photograph from a textbook or overhead transparency, or an image using a flexi cam attached between a microscope and television screen. If you have access to a computer and projector, there are good images of cells on CD-ROMs such as *Encarta*. Others can be accessed and downloaded from the Internet. It is well worth searching the Internet for recent video clips, flash animation and so on. These can be saved for future use so, although the initial searching process may be time-consuming, you can build up a good stock of interesting material.

I stress the need for clean, unbroken lines for all outlines and double lines for the cell walls to illustrate that they have thickness. I start by very lightly sketching the overall shape of the cell, making sure that it is in proportion and occupies between a quarter and half of the space I have available (the rest will be used for labels, title and magnification). I then fill in faint outlines of the main features I wish to include. When I am happy that the details are the correct shape and in proportion, I make a final outline, rubbing out any of the light sketching as I go along. Any labels should be outside the drawing, written horizontally, linked by ruled pencil lines and touching the part they are identifying. I emphasise that label lines should never cross each other. When adding the magnification of the drawing, a certain amount of estimation is needed. I stress that the magnification is only for guidance and never intended to be too precise. I start by working out the magnification of the microscope, then multiply this by the approximate enlargement I have made in drawing the object. Finally, each drawing should have a title. Details such as the way the section was cut (transversely or longitudinally) should be included when appropriate.

Your syllabus will identify if drawing skills are required for practical examinations. For example, in the CIE IGCSE Biology (0610) practical paper, students may be required to carry out an exercise that involves making a line drawing of a specimen, indicating the magnification of the drawing and labelling it. In the same syllabus, the Alternative to practical (Paper 6) requires students to be able to make clear drawings from a photograph of a specimen, indicating the magnification of the drawing and labelling it.

Do encourage the use of annotation in drawings. This helps students to relate features to their adaptations and functions as well as reducing the need for extended notes.

Making measurements

The key issue in experiments is the *validity* of the data obtained. This data must be relevant to the issue being studied. In other words, the dependent variable must be affected by the independent variable and not by some other factor that the experimenter has not considered or controlled. The instrument being used to collect the data must, therefore, be selected for its ability to measure the independent variable.

Measuring skills are involved both in setting up experiments and in monitoring the outcomes. *Accuracy* is vital if the results are to be reliable. In an investigation, students should have the freedom to select appropriate measuring instruments and they should be able to justify their choice.

For example, in the osmosis investigation, a student is likely to require 20 cm^3 of a range of sugar solutions. You could provide a choice of a 100 cm^3 beaker and a range of measuring cylinders of different sizes (10 cm^3, 25 cm^3, 50 cm^3). Other, more accurate instruments may be considered (e.g. mouth pipettes, but cost or safety could be a limiting factor here). These points could always be raised in the student's evaluation of the investigation. The level of accuracy recorded needs to be appropriate to the factor that is being measured. In this case, while the 10 cm^3 measuring cylinder may give the most accurate measurement, the time involved in measuring out numerous 20 cm^3 samples – filling the cylinder twice for each sample – would be impracticable. Using the 25 cm^3 cylinder would be most appropriate for this task.

In another example, involving the measurement of pulse rate, although a stopwatch will routinely give time to one hundredth of a second, accuracy to the nearest second is appropriate. Your students need to be encouraged to record measurements to the appropriate number of decimal places. On the other hand, they must not round up or round down results, arbitrarily removing decimal places, if it risks reducing the reliability of the data.

One example of an investigation where students can make measurements with a limited amount of specialised apparatus is associated with the topic of friction (see Student activity 7.1).

Student activity 7.1

Resources per group:
- wooden block, large enough to hold a range of weights, with a hook at one side;
- newton meter;
- range of different weights;
- range of surfaces, e.g. carpet or carpet tile, sandpaper, plastic, wood.

Students choose whether to investigate the effect on the friction force of:
(a) the weight of the object;
(b) the type of surface (probably the easier option).

For (a), attach the newton meter to the wooden block. Record the force needed to start the block moving with different load weights placed on it. Students should be encouraged to make a fair test by recognising that the type of surface must be kept the same throughout the investigation.

For (b), attach the newton meter to the wooden block. Place a weight on the block. Record the force needed to start the block moving on different surfaces. Students should be encouraged to make a fair test by recognising that the load weight must be kept the same throughout the investigation.

Do go back to basics when introducing classes to the skills of measuring: re-emphasise how to measure liquids in a measuring cylinder, pointing out the need to make sure the base of the meniscus is at eye level to avoid parallax error. Check that they are aware that water has a meniscus. Stress how the presence of a meniscus can result in mis-readings. Remind students that the ends of most rulers have a short section with no readings on, so it is important to place the zero mark against the start of what you intend to measure.

Measurements can be judgemental. For example, in the Chemistry investigation to study the rate of reaction between sodium thiosulphate and hydrochloric acid, the time taken for the cross beneath the reaction vessel to disappear from view is noted. The student has to decide when the cross has disappeared, before stopping the stopwatch. No matter how accurate the stopwatch may be, the student's judgement will affect the reliability of the data. When comparing sets of results collected by a number of groups, this point can be discussed effectively. It forms the basis for arguing that a set of results should all be collected by the same person, rather than different individuals taking turns. I have found this to be a particular problem with enzyme experiments, when the end point is indicated by the lack of blue-black colouration on a spotting tile (due to the complete breakdown of starch by amylase). Different individuals can produce wildly differing results, despite using the same chemicals in the same conditions.

Collecting duplicate sets of data is normally encouraged (although it is not always possible, due to time constraints or limited supplies of apparatus or chemicals). Means can then be calculated later. Students should compare these sets as they collect them: if two readings for the same condition show too much variation, the student should be encouraged to take a third or fourth reading. Only then can they be sure the results are reliable. I will discuss this issue in more detail in Chapter 11.

Identify a piece of practical work you intend to carry out with a class of students to support the theory you are teaching them. For this practical activity, make a point of emphasising to your class what observations will need to be made and the sort of detail required. If measurements are involved, discuss to what accuracy these should be made and what units will be used.

LOOKING BACK

Making observations and measurements are very important practical skills.

◆ How can you ensure that your students have the opportunities to practise different types of observation? Is there scope for you to extend your practicals to give them more practice?

◆ Are your students confident in their drawing ability? How can you encourage them?

◆ How can you guide your students to consider accuracy of measurement when choosing apparatus?

8 Recording observations and measurements

All too often, usually due to a lack of adequate guidelines or instructions, students fail to make adequate records or details of the observations and measurements they make. They may not record them at all ('I'll remember them for next lesson') or fail to note details adequately, overlooking the most obvious or significant points.

For example, I was teaching a new unit that my department had developed, on variation within species, to a group of lower ability 12-year-olds. I decided that an interesting way to approach the topic would be to give the students a selection of different varieties of apple to compare. I expected the class to record details such as colour, smell, size, taste etc. On my suggestion, a colleague had tried the same exercise with a difficult class, but had abandoned it when a few students disrupted the practical by eating all the samples, before the rest could make their observations. (We all have the occasional disaster!)

I decided, in the light of his experience, to structure the exercise more carefully. I organised the class into groups of four, each with their own table to work on to minimise movement. One student from each group was given responsibility for the apple sample. Each group was given a different variety of apple – one whole, labelled apple plus a plastic cup of apple pieces to use as a taste test. The pieces were in water to slow down the browning process. I gave what I thought were clear instructions – describe the apple, completing a table (drawn on the whiteboard) to record observations, then swap samples with other groups until all samples had been observed by all the groups. However, because I had described the activity as a taste test, the students focused on this and overlooked the most obvious features (size, colour and smell). The texture of the apple was also generally ignored. I learned from the experience – I now list on the board the details that need to be included as observations, having discussed possible features with the class. For less able classes, I divide the observations column into subgroups to make sure the students make all the observations necessary to complete the exercise effectively. This practical has proved to be a very popular lesson – normally we have to insist on no eating, drinking or chewing in the laboratory!

There is no harm in carrying out this sort of activity – if safety risks have been assessed and hazards minimised (chemicals are moved away from food, surfaces are clean and so on) and, in terms of resources, it is very inexpensive (the cost of five or six apples). I will discuss the conclusions of this practical in Chapter 10.

As classes become more experienced in recording observations, the guidelines you have to give them should reduce, allowing them to become more self-reliant and to develop their own initiative. This will reflect on your teaching and the number of opportunities you have provided for your classes to develop this skill.

Using tables to record results
Preparation of results tables

Tables are very useful in the organising of results. Computers have made our lives much easier here. Data can be put into a table quite randomly and it is then very easy to sort it. Creating a table on paper is not quite so straightforward – it requires pre-planning and the data needs to be organised before the students enter it into the columns or rows. A table may run vertically or horizontally, depending on the number of observations made and the number of categories required.

Example of a horizontal table

Table 8.1 is used to display the results from a practical to compare the diffusion of dilute and concentrated ammonia.

Table 8.1: Times for concentrated and dilute ammonia to move along a glass tube

Distance along tube (cm)	0	10	12	14	16	18	20	22	24	26	28	30
Time for conc. NH_3 (s)												
Time for dil. NH_3 (s)												

I usually run this practical as a demonstration and it is appropriate in either Chemistry or Biology as a model to show the effect of concentration on rate of diffusion. Two wide glass tubes (between 40 cm and 50 cm long) are set up prior to the demonstration. (I note that some textbooks recommend a tube of up to 100 cm long. This is, in my opinion, excessive: it is extremely difficult to set up, more likely to get broken and will take literally hours before dilute ammonia will diffuse from one end to the other. Results collected over a distance of 40 cm are more than adequate for comparison. Even then, dilute ammonia may take more than 40 minutes to diffuse this distance.) Marks are painted with white paint or white correction fluid on the surface every 2 cm on the glass tube, starting at 10 cm from one end. Pieces of damp red litmus are inserted, using a glass rod, at each 2 cm mark. The dampness of the litmus is sufficient for them to stick to the wall of the tube. Two cork stoppers are needed for each glass tube. One of each pair has its end scooped out slightly to allow some cotton wool to be pressed in. Both glass tubes are clamped horizontally and stoppers are inserted in the far end of each. The cotton wool is saturated with (a) dilute ammonia solution; and (b) concentrated ammonia solution. As soon as the stopper is placed in the glass tube, a stopwatch is started. The time taken for each piece of litmus paper to start turning blue is noted. I run both tubes simultaneously, with two groups of students being put in charge of observing and recording, while the rest of the class write up a method, draw a diagram of the apparatus and create the results table.

Example of a vertical table

Table 8.2 gives results of an osmosis investigation to find out the effect of a range of sugar solutions on the size of potato sticks.

Table 8.2: Results of osmosis investigation

Concentration of sugar solution (mol/dm^3)	Length of potato at start (mm)	Length of potato after 24 hours (mm)		Mean length (mm)	Mean change in length (mm)	Percentage change in length
		Piece 1	Piece 2			
0.0	60	60	64	62.0	+2.0	+3.3
0.2	60	58	59	58.5	−1.5	−2.5
0.4	60	55	55	55.0	−5.0	−8.3
0.6	60	54	54	54.0	−6.0	−10.0
0.8	60	53	54	53.5	−6.5	−10.8
1.0	60	52	53	52.5	−7.5	−12.5

I run this as a whole class investigation, with students required to plan the investigation, selecting the equipment, predicting the likely outcomes and carrying out their method individually (or in small groups to pool results if equipment is limited). Stock solutions of sugar, ranging from 0.0 mol/dm^3 (distilled water) to 1.0 mol/dm^3, are made available so that there is an element of choice. Students need to be able to identify variables and plan to control them.

Table format

When starting a course, students will need to be provided with a table framework (i.e. the basic outline of the table, with headings, columns and rows, into which they insert their results), but they should be given opportunities to design their own tables with suitable headings and units. For the highest scores in coursework that is assessed by schools (e.g. skill C2 in IGCSE Biology (0610)), students need to be able to record results in an appropriate manner, designing the format themselves.

Title

This should describe the relationship that the data in the table represents, for example 'Table to show the effect of changing the concentration of sugar solution on the length of potato pieces'.

Table headings

As a teacher, you need to emphasise to your students the need to put adequate detail into the table headings. This should describe what the data in the column represents (the physical quantity) and should state, where appropriate, the units used in the measurement. All too often, students ignore units completely or write them after each individual result.

Units used in the table should be appropriate. The syllabus you teach will have a list of recommended units, with names and symbols. Two good sources of information are Association of Science Education (ASE) (1995) and Institute of Biology (2000). These publications are used by Principal Examiners for reference when setting papers. Students need to be familiar with the standard terms, units and symbols, and should use them as a matter of routine during practical work. You could issue students with a glossary of these at the beginning of the course, so they have a ready source of reference.

There are four acceptable ways of stating some units. Speed, for example, could be written as 'metres per second', 'm per s', 'm/s' or 'm s^{-1}'. Once a student has the correct column headings and units, it will make life much easier during graph construction, since these can be transferred directly to the axes of the graph.

Unfortunately, units have changed over the years, so older textbooks may quote units that are no longer acceptable. Ones to watch out for include those used in imperial measurements: the International System (SI) is now the standard. Also, calories are obsolete – joules (J) and kilojoules (kJ) are the accepted units for energy. Note that calories can be converted to joules by multiplying the value by 4.2. The cubic decimetre (dm^3) is preferred to the litre. The cubic centimetre (cm^3) is preferred to the millilitre (ml).

Table columns

The columns are normally separated with a line drawn using a ruler. The first column in a vertical table (or row in a horizontal table) should contain the data collected for the independent variable (also known as the input variable). The values for this data normally increase by even amounts, chosen by the experimenter. They should be written in rank order – smallest to largest or vice versa. The second column should contain the observations or measurements made – the dependent, or output, variable. If repeat sets of data have been collected, these are then displayed in subsequent columns. Where repeats have been made, it is common practice to process these using some form of calculation (a mean, change in length, percentage change etc.). This derived data is displayed in further columns.

Another important detail is in recording each piece of data to the same number of decimal places. This indicates that all the data has been collected to the same degree of accuracy.

A good way of emphasising how to construct an acceptable table is in giving students examples of poorly constructed tables and asking them to identify the shortfalls in them. It is also important to stress that the skill of table construction may be tested in practical examinations and also in written papers.

Using drawings to record results

Observations may be recorded in the form of diagrams – labelled or annotated. I have already discussed sketching diagrams in Chapter 7. Generally, students are very poor at annotating diagrams. They will often spend time revising labelled diagrams and then include these in extended answers to examination questions. However, these rarely add value to the answer (unless the question has specifically asked for a diagram) due to lack of annotation to bring the features drawn into the context of the question.

Student activity 8.1

The table shown opposite was produced by a student teacher to record the results of an experiment to compare the breathing rates of two pupils running a race. I now use it with classes to identify faults in table construction.

TIME FROM START	BREATHING RATE OF STUDENT 1	BREATHING RATE OF STUDENT 2
0 mins	16	18
30 seconds	18	20
1 min	21	23
1 min 30 secs	25	27
2 mins	30	32
2 mins 30 secs	31	35
3 mins	31	35
3 mins 30 secs	24	33
4 mins	20	30
4 mins 30 secs	16	26

The features your class will identify may include lack of units in the heading for time, use of capital letters and underlining in the headings, use of two units for time (minutes and seconds) and lack of units for breathing rate (which should be breaths per minute).

You could then ask the class to produce a corrected version of the table, and plot the results on a graph with both sets on the same axes, using corrected column headings to label the axes.

Teacher activity 8.1

Modify Student activity 8.1, using other data and headings to make a similar example for a different topic in Biology, or for Chemistry or Physics.

LOOKING BACK

- How do you make sure that students write down observations and measurements as they make them?
- What guidance do you provide to help your students decide what to observe or measure?

9 Handling data

Once the data has been collected, decisions need to be made about how to process it to make meaningful comparisons, to identify trends and to form conclusions. Calculations may be required and the results may be plotted in a graph.

Teacher activity 9.1

Go through past papers to collect a set of examples of data handling. Put these together in the form of a booklet to use with a class to reinforce the skills they may need to demonstrate in an examination. There may be other questions associated with the data. These could be cut so that they do not appear in the booklet, or left on if the students are nearing the end of the syllabus. The other parts of the question could then form part of the revision process.

If you do not have copies of past papers, contact your exam board to order them.

Calculations

The principal types of calculation that students will be expected to do include calculating:
- means;
- change;
- percentage change.

Calculating means

A mean is the average of a group of values. It is calculated by adding together all the values and then dividing by the number of individual values. Where repeat sets of data have been collected, the means should give a representative picture. However, it is important to consider the validity of the results at this stage. It is almost impossible to get exactly the same result for each repeat reading – all the variables involved would have to be kept the same, human error would have to be eliminated and accuracy in measuring would need to be perfect. However, the raw data is still important since it shows the variation in the data collected for each set of repeated readings. A large variation between individual results collected as repeats would suggest that they were not very reliable. However, a number of similar results and one very different result (an outlier) would indicate that the results were reliable apart from that single one, which could then be ignored. See Tables 8.2 and 10.2 for examples of calculating means (averages).

Calculating change

This enables us to compare measurements at the start and end of the experiment, or at points during its progress, to determine what difference has been caused. This is acceptable, so long as there is the same starting point in each case. However, it is not always possible to have the same starting point. For example, it may not be possible to begin with exactly the same mass of a chemical compound each time, particularly if a very sensitive top pan balance is used. In this case, the change is not adequate; we need to go one stage further and calculate the percentage change. See Tables 8.2 and 10.2 for an example of the use of the calculation of change.

Calculating percentage change

This takes into account differences in the starting point (mass, length, temperature etc.) so that a comparison of the changes will be valid. It is calculated by dividing the change in the quantity by the original amount and then multiplying by 100. Students often need to be reminded that percentages do not have units. See Table 8.2 for an example of the use of the calculation of percentage change.

Other calculations

These will depend on the subject area. Often, the results are put into a formula to convert them to another value, e.g. speed, resistance, reaction rate, energy. Table 10.1 contains data that has been converted into a rate.

Plotting graphs

In addition to calculations, data is usually processed into graphs. The type of graph selected depends on the nature of the data collected, but any graph should have a title that describes what the graph represents. All but pie charts need axes with labels that include units, where appropriate (these can be taken directly from the headings in the results table). The independent variable is normally plotted on the horizontal x-axis and the dependent variable is plotted on the vertical y-axis. Students often have difficulty identifying which is which. I tell them that, of the pair of readings they are plotting, they have chosen which values to give one of the quantities. This is the independent variable and it usually goes along the x-axis. For example, when producing an extension–load graph, the student has chosen to measure the load in 0, 1, 2, 3 newtons and so on, so this is the independent variable and forms the x-axis.

Do insist that students use a pencil and ruler to plot graphs. Mistakes can then be easily rectified.

Students need to be encouraged to decide what type of graph is appropriate. Options include:
- pie charts;
- bar charts;
- histograms;
- line and scatter graphs.

Teacher activity 9.2

Design a decision table to help students select the appropriate type of graph for their data.

Pie charts

These are used occasionally in Science where the data is easily divided into fractions or percentages and students wish to compare the relative proportions. A pie chart is useful for displaying information such as the content of different foodstuffs (protein, fat, carbohydrate, water and fibre) in a typical diet or food, or looking at the range and proportions of variation of a characteristic, such as eye colour. In the case shown in Table 9.1, the class contained 25 students, making the conversion of frequencies into percentages very straightforward.

Table 9.1: Eye colour data

Eye colour	Number of students	Percentage of total
Blue	11	44
Brown	7	28
Hazel	4	16
Green	3	12

The size of the sectors is worked out using a pie chart scale or a protractor (for percentages, 3 degrees represent 1%). The chart should be drawn with the sectors in rank order, largest first, beginning at the top (12 o'clock) and proceeding clockwise, as shown in Figure 9.1. A pie chart, like any other form of graph, needs a meaningful title. Each sector is usually shaded or coloured, with a key to show what it represents. Again, computer programs can make the plotting of these quite straightforward and do not reduce the value of the work. In addition, they allow students to focus on the data analysis part of the investigation.

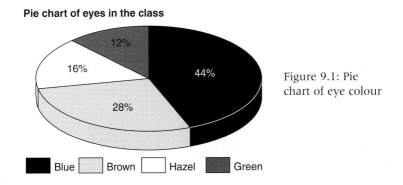

Pie chart of eyes in the class

Figure 9.1: Pie chart of eye colour

Bar charts

If either the independent or dependent variable is categoric (distinct categories, for example eye colour) rather than numerical, then a bar chart would be appropriate. The horizontal axis is a list of categories and the blocks are of equal width, separated from each other by a space, with equal spacing between each block. The example shown in Figure 9.2 is not based on data a class could collect, but students should be able to handle data from secondary sources to develop their practical skills.

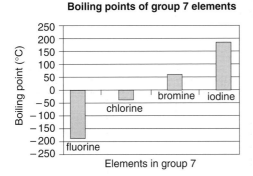

Boiling points of group 7 elements

Figure 9.2: Bar chart to show the boiling points of group 7 elements (the halogens)

Histograms

For a continuous (numerical) characteristic such as height, the frequencies of different values are shown using a form of histogram. This is slightly different from a bar chart since each of the blocks touches the next. The blocks should be drawn in order of either increasing or decreasing magnitude, as shown in Figure 9.3. While a normal distribution would be ideal, this graph shows more typical class results! The two peaks are probably present because the sample contained both boys and girls. Students need to be encouraged to avoid overlapping ranges, using, for example, 1–10, 11–20, rather than 1–10, 10–20 etc. Otherwise, values can be placed in more than one category.

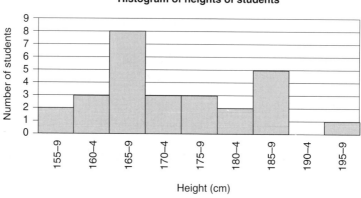

Figure 9.3: Histogram to show variation in height of students in a class

Line and scatter graphs

If both variables are continuous then line graphs or scatter graphs can be plotted. Each point plotted should be clearly marked as a cross (×) or as an encircled dot (⊙). If a further curve is included, vertical crosses (+) may be used to mark the points. Graphs plotted using computer programs have equal value to those plotted free hand. However, if the graph is plotted using a computer program such as Microsoft Excel, the points may have to be different, since the options recommended above are not available. For line graphs, the points should be joined. Strictly, this is called a 'curve' – whether it is straight or curved!

Students often lack confidence in drawing curved lines. I encourage my students to use their elbow as a pivot to produce an arc. If necessary, turn the paper so that the x-axis is at the top, to achieve the curve required. First, pass the pencil above the paper without touching, practising the curve. Gradually, sweep across the paper and touch it, leaving a lightly drawn line. If is unsatisfactory, the line is easily rubbed out and another attempt can be made. Once the correct curve has been sketched, go over it with a clear, unbroken line and rub out any sketching.

Encourage your students to draw a line of best fit. This is best drawn free hand – even on a graph that has been produced on computer. The best-fit line should pass through the majority of points, with an approximately equal number on either side of the curve. Transparent rulers are useful when the best-fit line is a straight line, since you can see the points through the ruler.

While the x-axis is usually plotted along the base of the graph paper, data can occasionally contain negative values, resulting in the x-axis being higher up the paper. Examples of this include the boiling points of the halogens, in Figure 9.2, and the effects of varying sugar concentration on length of potato pieces, as illustrated in Figure 9.4.

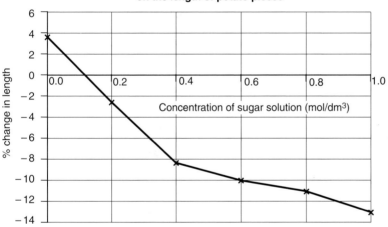

Figure 9.4: Example of a line graph with positive and negative values for the x-axis

Note that the graph shown above is not ideal, since the line is computer generated and is not a curve – and therefore not strictly a line of best fit.

Students tend to plot the means where they have been calculated, but it is sometimes useful to plot all the data, generally on a scatter graph, since this shows the amount of variation within each set of repeats. This provides a point of discussion in the evaluation of the investigation.

Tables 9.2a to 9.2c (Biology, Chemistry and Physics, respectively) give examples of a range of experiments and the types of graph the data from them would generate.

Table 9.2a: Examples of experiments and the graphs that would result from them: Biology

	Independent (input) variable	Dependent (output) variable	Type of graph
Comparing the energy in different types of nut	type of nut	energy released	bar chart
Comparing the energy in nuts of different sizes	mass of nut	energy released	line graph
Comparing the number of students in the class who can/cannot roll their tongues	ability to roll tongue (yes/no)	number of students	bar chart or pie chart
Studying variation in height of students in the class	height	number of students (frequency)	histogram
Effect of temperature on an enzyme-controlled reaction	temperature	rate of reaction	line graph

Table 9.2b: Examples of experiments and the graphs that would result from them: Chemistry

	Independent (input) variable	Dependent (output) variable	Type of graph
Melting points of metals in group 1 of the periodic table	name of metal	melting point	bar chart
Comparing how long a candle burns in small, medium and large jars	size of jar	time before the candle goes out	bar chart
Comparing the effect of beaker volume on how long a candle burns	volume of beaker	time before the candle goes out	line graph
Comparing the energy released by burning different types of fuel	type of fuel	energy released	bar chart

Table 9.2c: Examples of experiments and the graphs that would result from them: Physics

	Independent (input) variable	Dependent (output) variable	Type of graph
Effect of changing the length of a wire on its resistance	length of wire	resistance	line graph
Cooling of water in a beaker insulated by a range of different materials	time	temperature of the water	line graph (with a different line plotted for each material, on the same axes)
	material	time to cool by a certain amount	bar chart
Monitoring the radioactive decay of iodine-128	time	count rate	line graph
Studying the relationship between voltage and the power of an electromagnet	voltage	number of paper clips attracted	histogram

LOOKING BACK

In this chapter I have emphasised that raw data usually needs to be processed to be able to interpret what it shows.

◆ How do you guide students towards the most useful calculations for their data?

◆ How do you help students choose the type of graph to plot?

10 Drawing conclusions

Drawing conclusions is a skill that involves analysing the results of the practical, stating and explaining what they show. A conclusion can be broken down into four parts, depending on the type of practical work. These involve:

- describing the processed results (often shown in graph form);
- looking for patterns and trends shown by the results;
- using scientific knowledge and understanding to explain the findings;
- referring back to a prediction or the problem set, explaining to what extent the conclusion supports the prediction or solves the problem.

As with other practical skills, I tend to give my students checklists so that they can make sure they have included all the relevant stages in their conclusion. You can find an example in Worksheet 10 (Appendix D).

Describing processed results

This may involve making a simple statement like 'When I reacted lumps of calcium carbonate with the acid, they reacted slower than powdered calcium carbonate.' This shows that the student has considered the collected evidence. Practical work does not always produce trends and results are not always quantitative. Food tests, for instance, do not necessarily generate patterns. A summary of the results may be all that needs to be stated. Students may only need to group together foods that give the same result. For example, 'Bread, rice, potato and pasta are all starchy foods because they turned blue-black with iodine solution.' In Physics, students may need to identify which materials are good and bad conductors of heat.

In the practical involving variation in apples, described in Chapter 8, students were required to put five apples in order according to their taste, from sweetest to most sour. With this investigation, I decided to convert qualitative results into quantitative ones by asking the students to give each apple a score from 5 for the sweetest to 1 for the least sweet (sourest). This made drawing a conclusion much easier for them.

Looking for patterns and trends

Graphs are very useful here because they give a visual representation of the results, making any relationship between the variables more obvious. Many investigations produce results that generate straight-line graphs. These show a relatively simple relationship. The student can then state this relationship. For example, a student investigating Hooke's Law, using a spring onto which increasing loads had been added, may conclude:

My graph is a straight line. This shows that as I increase the load on the spring, its extension increases.

Your students should be encouraged to support their conclusions with data they have collected. Therefore, an improvement on the previous conclusion would be:

My graph is a straight line. This shows that as I increase the load on the spring, its extension increases. For example, a load of 2 N produced an extension of 20 mm. A load of 4 N produced an extension of 40 mm. As I doubled the load, the extension doubled.

This investigation generates a graph in which the variables are directly proportional to each other (until the yield point is reached): the graph is a straight line, passing through the origin (0, 0). Your students may develop such terms in Mathematics as well as through your teaching in Science, and you should encourage their use in conclusions. This relationship – direct proportionality – is not always apparent in a set of results: it depends on how they have been processed.

For example, Table 10.1 shows the results of an experiment to study the effect of concentration on a reaction.

Table 10.1: Results of an experiment to study the effect of concentration on a reaction

Concentration of sodium thiosulphate (g/dm^3)	Average time for cross to disappear (s)	Rate of reaction (s^{-1}) $\times 10^{-3}$
40	27.5	36.36
32	38.5	25.97
24	48.0	20.83
16	81.0	12.35
8	152.0	6.58

If the student measures the time the reaction takes at different concentrations and then plots this data, a curve is generated, as shown in Figure 10.1.

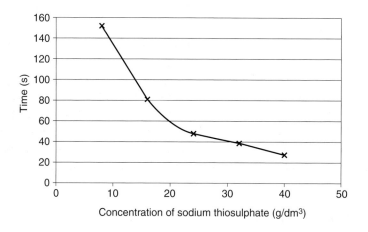

Figure 10.1: The effect of concentration on the time a reaction takes

However, if the rate is calculated using the formula: rate $= \frac{1}{t}$, then a straight-line graph is produced when concentration against rate is plotted (see Figure 10.2).

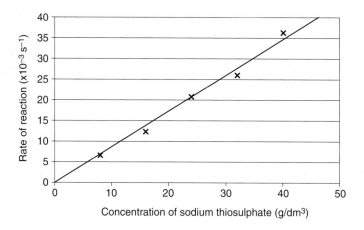

Figure 10.2: The effect of concentration on rate of reaction

Both graphs are correct, but the pattern shown in the second graph is much easier for the student to describe in a conclusion. However, converting times to rates can generate data that is less easy to handle, particularly if the graph is being plotted on paper rather than using a computer program, so you need to decide how and when to do this with your students.

It is worth noting that converting times to rates does not always produce straight-line graphs. Plotting data from investigations involving temperature as the fixed variable can produce curves. For example, in enzyme experiments, the rate of reaction doubles for every 10 °C rise in temperature until the reaction nears the optimum temperature, giving a curve. At around the optimum, the increase in rate slows down, so the line of the graph forms a plateau. Further rises in temperature result in a decrease in rate as the enzyme molecules begin to denature.

Using scientific knowledge and understanding

It is important that your students are able to apply the knowledge and understanding they have developed to explain the findings of an investigation: they need to be able to state, in scientific terms, why the results show a pattern or trend.

Example of a conclusion containing a scientific explanation

Background

Students were asked to carry out an investigation to see if there is a relationship between the size of a peanut and the amount of energy in it. This was carried out at the end of a unit on nutrition. They already knew how to measure the energy in food by burning it under a boiling tube containing water. They were given the formula to convert temperature changes into energy figures:

energy (joules) = mass of water (g) $\times$ temperature change (°C) $\times$ 4.2

A student's results table and graph derived from the data are shown in Table 10.2 and Figure 10.3 to put his conclusion in context.

Table 10.2 Results of investigation into the relationship between the size of a peanut and the energy in it

Mass of nut (g)	Temperature of water (°C)		Change in temperature (°C)	Energy released (J)	Mean energy (J)
	At start	At end			
0.3	19	29	10	1050	1240
0.3	19	45	26	1430	
0.5	21	43	22	2310	2835
0.5	21	53	32	3360	
0.7	19	57	38	3990	3885
0.7	19	59	36	3780	
0.8	19	59	40	4200	4300
0.8	18	60	42	4400	
1.0	19	81	62	6510	5932
1.0	20	71	51	5355	

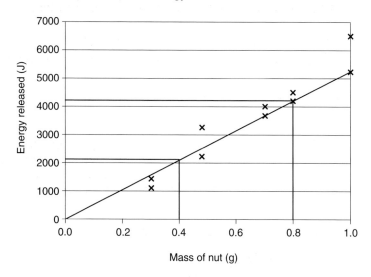

Graph to show the energy released from different sized nuts

Figure 10.3: The relationship between mass of nut and the energy released from it

Conclusion

As I increased the mass of the nut, the amount of energy released increased. All my average results show this pattern. For example, from my graph, a nut weighing 0.4 g will release 2100 J. A nut of double that mass (0.8 g) will release 4200 J. So, as I double the size of the nut, the amount of energy released doubles. The amount of heat released when I burn a nut is directly proportional to its mass. Not all my results show this pattern – I know some are anomalous because they are not near my line of best fit (e.g. the first nut at 1.0 g gave out more heat than expected and the nuts weighing 0.3 g seem to give out less heat than they should have done), but most points are on or near the curve. My results are what I expected, since nuts contain fat, which burns to release heat energy. A large nut should contain twice as much fat as a nut half its size, so the large nut will release twice as much heat.

This student also went on to comment on the possible causes of the anomalous results and to make suggestions about overcoming these if he had the chance to extend the investigation, as part of his evaluation.

Referring back to a prediction or the problem set

The student may have begun the investigation with a statement about what they wanted to find out (defining the problem) or with a prediction (what the expected outcome would be). This last section of the conclusion links back to this statement. Similarities and differences between the prediction (if there is one) may be discussed to bring the quality of the conclusion to a high level. It may be appropriate to revisit any theory used at the planning stage of the investigation to support the conclusion.

Example of a student's conclusion to a Chemistry investigation

This is based on two graphs (Figures 10.4 and 10.5) plotted from her results.

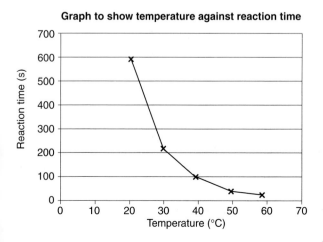

Graph to show temperature against reaction time

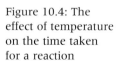

Figure 10.4: The effect of temperature on the time taken for a reaction

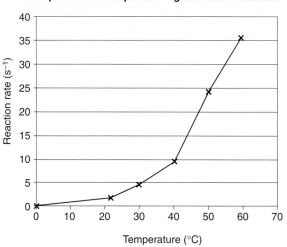

Graph to show temperature against rate of reaction

Figure 10.5: The effect of temperature on the rate of a reaction

Conclusion

The results show that as the temperature increases, the time taken for the reaction decreases but the rate of reaction increases. This is clearly shown on both graphs.

The results back up my prediction that, as the temperature of reaction increases, so will the rate of reaction. As stated in my prediction, this is because as the temperature increases, the particles get more kinetic energy. This means they move around faster and so more successful collisions take place. The reactions therefore have more energy so the Ea (activation energy) is overcome more easily. However, in my prediction I stated that as the temperature doubled the rate of reaction would also double. From the graph, it can be seen that this is not the case. For every 10 °C gained, the rate of reaction appears to double. For example, at 20 °C the rate of reaction was 1.7 s^{-1} (X 10^3), and at 30°C the rate of reaction was 4.4 s^{-1} (X 10^3).

Comment

The scientific detail given by this student goes well beyond IGCSE level. It supports the conclusion well and takes into consideration aspects that don't support the initial prediction.

The development of the skill of forming conclusions is not limited to doing the practical work. Students need as much practice as possible. Student activity 10.1 is one strategy I use to develop this skill.

Student activity 10.1

I collect sets of results that classes have produced and use these for class tasks and homework involving the interpretation of data from secondary sources. I give a brief background to the results, putting them into context (the purpose of the experiment, how the results were collected). Then I set a task. This may be calculating means or percentage changes if I have presented a table in an incomplete form, plotting a graph, drawing a line of best fit and writing a conclusion. I may set a number of questions that draw out the conclusion from the results. This is, effectively, a writing frame. Less able students are able to put together valid conclusions when given some structure. It makes the task accessible to them because it breaks it down into manageable stages.

Teacher activity 10.1

Collect a set of graphs for your subject. You could use examples from this book, other textbooks or a range produced by your own students. They could be printed out and photocopied, or scanned into a computer and printed onto overhead transparencies for whole group work.

Student activity 10.2

When teaching a class about drawing conclusions, use the graphs gathered in Teacher activity 10.1 as teaching aids. Instruct the class to interpret each graph to form the basis for a conclusion. You may need to put each graph into context first.

LOOKING BACK

Students cope better with writing conclusions when they are broken into more easily manageable stages.

◆ How can you help your students write full and coherent conclusions?
◆ Do you use writing frames to help less able students?

11 Evaluation

Evaluating tends to be the skill that students find most difficult. This skill can be defined as judging the validity of conclusions by considering the quality of the evidence and the suitability of the procedure. It therefore involves judging the accuracy of measuring and the reliability of the data collected. In IGCSE syllabuses, if students are producing coursework for assessment, it is associated with consideration of the planning stage (C4) of an investigation. Here, students are required to:

- comment critically on their original plan;
- evaluate chosen procedures;
- suggest/implement modifications where appropriate;
- show a systematic approach to dealing with unexpected results.

So the evaluation may take place either during the practical, resulting in the implementation of modifications, and/or at the end of the practical – after the data has been handled and conclusions have been made. The evaluation may involve:

- commenting on how successfully a plan was implemented;
- suggestions for improvements if the investigation was going to be rerun;
- comparing repeated results to consider their similarity and, hence, considering the reliability of the evidence;
- identification of what might have caused a reading to be incorrect or unreliable;
- stating the importance of collecting extra results where a piece of data already collected does not fit the expected trend;
- considering the accuracy of the apparatus used for making measurements and suggesting alternatives where appropriate;
- considering how appropriate the apparatus used in the investigation was and suggesting improvements (if alternative apparatus is available);
- analysing data on a graph to identify anomalous results;
- commenting on how well the evidence supports the conclusion;
- considering extra variables not identified in the planning stage and suggesting how these may be controlled;

- suggesting further work using the same technique to provide additional relevant evidence;
- suggesting a different technique that might be used to investigate the same idea;
- comparing the results collected with secondhand evidence (such as a graph in a textbook) to consider whether the evidence can be trusted or not.

Worksheet 11(Appendix D) shows an example of an evaluation checklist I use with my students. You could modify this to suit the requirements of the syllabus you follow.

This chapter gives three example evaluations that will give you an idea of the quality that a high-achieving student can produce. It is worthwhile presenting weaker examples of evaluations to your students, putting the work in context and asking the class to suggest ways of making improvements.

Example 1: The effect of light intensity on rate of photosynthesis in a water plant
Background
Some water plants will produce bubbles of oxygen from cut stems as they photosynthesise. A student has used the apparatus shown in Figure 11.1. There are various possible ways of doing this investigation (see Freeland (1987: 42–3), Pickering (2000: 150–1) or Mackean (2002: 38) for alternative approaches).

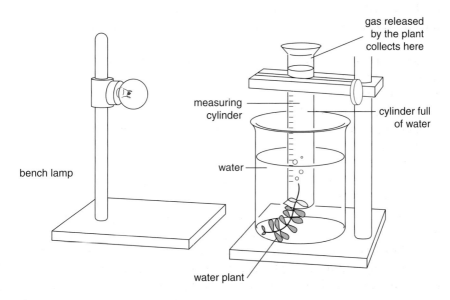

Figure 11.1: Apparatus to measure rate of photosynthesis in a pond plant

The bench lamp has been used as the light source. It has been moved to various distances away from the plant to vary light intensity. The student took a bubble count over a fixed period of time at each distance in order to get a measurement of the photosynthetic rate.

Evaluation

I only took one reading for each distance. If I had more time I would take at least two. The second reading should be similar to the first if they are reliable. I used the number of bubbles produced in a minute to measure rate of photosynthesis. But, I noticed that the bubbles were not all the same size, so 20 bubbles in one reading might actually be a faster rate than 20 bubbles in another reading. If I could do the experiment again, a better way to measure the rate might be to collect the gas bubbles in a container that gives me a volume. I could use a measuring cylinder, upside down and full of water, like I did in an enzyme experiment. This way, it would not matter what size the bubbles were — I would be measuring the total volume of bubbles collected in a minute.

Comments

This student has thought a lot about the method used. She has recognised that there were variables she did not control at the time (bubble size) and applied her experience of gas collection in a different practical (the effect of temperature on oxygen production by catalase in potato) to suggest improvements. Time is often a limiting factor in practicals such as this. Students may not have enough time to collect duplicate sets of results, but they should still plan to take them. If you decide that there will not be sufficient time to do this, you could ask groups of students to share results. Students should identify their own results in their work. However, with this investigation, different plants behave very differently so 'repeats' may not be comparable.

Another student in the same class noted that the lamp was producing heat as well as light. When the lamp was near the beaker with the plant in, the water could warm up. He modified his plan to test this out. He put a thermometer in the beaker and monitored the water temperature at each lamp distance from the beaker. In his evaluation he then discussed this, noting that the water warmed up when the bulb was close, so the increase in rate of gas production could be due to higher temperature as well as light intensity. He then stated that he could not rely on the results collected when the lamp was close. He was unable to suggest how to control this variable (a standard way is to have another beaker of water in between the lamp and the beaker containing the pond plant to absorb any heat).

Example 2: Effect of concentration on the rate of reaction between sodium thiosulphate solution and hydrochloric acid

Background

A range of concentrations of sodium thiosulphate can be set up by adding different volumes of the chemical with water to make up 50 cm³ of solution (see Table 11.1).

Table 11.1: Range of concentrations of sodium thiosulphate

Volume of 0.15 mol/dm³ sodium thiosulphate solution (cm³)	Volume of water (cm³)
50	0
40	10
30	20
20	30
10	40

Students can then calculate the concentration of each solution. At the planning stage, they should choose what dilutions to make up and what range they wish to use.

In this reaction, insoluble sulphur is produced, making the reaction mixture cloudy, so the cross disappears from view (see Figure 11.2). For each concentration of sodium thiosulphate, the time taken for the cross to disappear is noted.

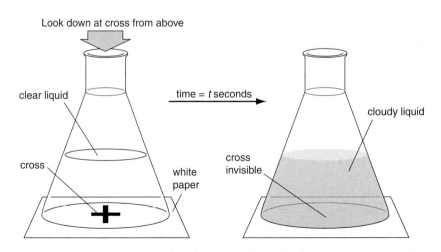

Figure 11.2: Apparatus to find out the effect of concentration of sodium thiosulphate on reaction rate (Source: Hunt and Sykes, 1984)

Evaluation

I had to stop the stopwatch when I couldn't see the cross any more. It was not easy to decide exactly when the cross had gone. I could improve the reliability of my results if I used a light sensor. This is what I would do. I will put a light over the conical flask so the light shines down through the liquid. I will put the light sensor under the flask. This will give me a reading of how much light is passing through the liquid. As the sulphur is produced, the liquid goes cloudy, so less light can get through to the sensor. I will time how long it takes the light to get completely blocked from the sensor.

Comments

This student has seen demonstrations using data logging equipment. Some Science departments have this equipment – perhaps sufficient for demonstrations, but not enough for whole class practical work. She was a particularly bright student who was interested in using data logging as a result of earlier work in the syllabus. The teacher prompted her to think about how she might apply prior experiences to improve this investigation. Prompts are fine – but beware of giving the student the answer!

More standard evaluations for this investigation involve:

- suggesting taking more repeat readings to check the validity of the results;
- using a wider range of concentrations to see if an extrapolation of the trend on a graph can be supported;
- using intermediate concentrations to provide more evidence to support the trend shown on a graph;
- suggesting reasons for why an anomalous result has happened and taking further readings to confirm what the correct reading should be;
- comparing the results with those shown in a textbook to see if the trend is the same;
- changing equipment named in the plan, such as the type of container to be used from, for example, a 250 cm^3 beaker to a 100 cm^3 conical flask, so that the depth of solution allows the cross to be obscured more quickly;
- changing the equipment needed to measure 5 cm^3 of hydrochloric acid, or the various volumes of sodium thiosulphate and water, to improve accuracy.

Example 3: The effect of current on an electromagnet
Background
This student has based an investigation on the equation:

$$B = \frac{\mu N I}{L}$$

where:
B = the magnetic field strength
μ = permeability of the core material
N = the number of turns
I = the current passing through the coils
L = length of the coil

He used the diagram shown in Figure 11.3, which he produced using a computer drawing package.

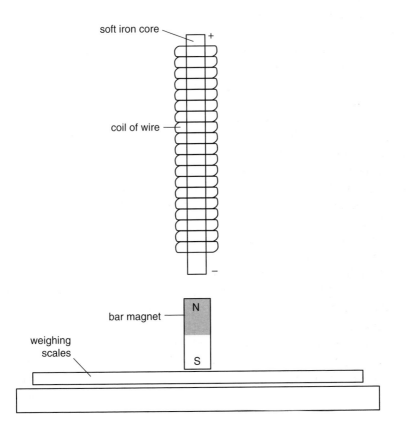

Figure 11.3: Apparatus to investigate the effect of current on an electromagnet

The data (reading on the 'weighing scales') was collected as the current in the coil was varied. As the current was increased, the electromagnet repelled the bar magnet more, increasing the reading on the 'weighing scales'.

Evaluation

I think that this was a fair experiment. The set-up was a very good way of carrying out the experiment, and gave accurate and reliable results. Because the dependent variables were kept the same throughout the experiment, no anomalous results were obtained. If the experiment was repeated I would use more current values, and use a more reliable power source because the one being used fluctuated slightly.

Other people in the class were investigating the same thing, but a different set-up was used, involving hanging weights off the electromagnet to see how much it could hold at different currents. For these experiments the same conclusion was reached that as the current increases so does the strength of the electromagnet. I am also sure that the conclusion is correct because in Co-ordinated Science – Physics by Stephen Pople and Peter Whitehead it states that 'Increasing the current makes the magnetic field stronger.'

Additional experiments that could be carried out to investigate electromagnets further would be to investigate what other factors affect the magnetic field strength. For example, an experiment could be carried out to investigate which core materials have the best permeability, or to see how changes in the number of coils affect the strength of the electromagnet.

Comments

This student has considered anomalous results (in this case, none). This statement is correct when comparing his average results: these produced a straight-line graph very well. However, there were significant variations in individual readings for the same current that he could have noted. He commented on the accuracy and reliability of the equipment used. He has suggested improvements and increasing the range of data collected. The student then compared his finding with those of other students in the class who had devised different approaches to the same investigation. Finally, he considered ways of extending the investigation to find out more about the properties of electromagnets.

Students tend to find the process of evaluating difficult. Study examples of writing frames such as that shown in Worksheets 2 and 3 (Appendix D) and design one for the evaluation of a specific investigation you use with a lower ability group. Reference to the evaluation checklist (Worksheet 11, Appendix D) may give you ideas about what questions to ask or instructions to give.

LOOKING BACK

The content of your students' evaluations will depend on the requirements of the syllabus you are teaching.

- How do you encourage students to comment critically on their own work?
- What can you do to help them identify weaknesses in their evaluation?

12 The assessment of practical skills

Students following any O Level or IGCSE Science course will face some form of examination of their practical skills. It is obviously very important that they develop good practical skills. Usually, 20% of the final examination mark will be derived from the demonstration of these, although the percentage may vary from one syllabus to another. Most syllabuses provide a choice of forms of assessment. Your Science department will need to decide on the most suitable option. The options are usually:

- **coursework**, which takes the form of school-based assessment of experimental skills and abilities;
- **practical test**, which is taken in examination conditions;
- **alternative to practical**, which is a written examination testing familiarity with laboratory-based procedures.

The choice that you or your department makes will depend on what laboratory facilities and range of equipment you have available.

In this chapter, I have included a range of examples of students' work to provide you with examples of the type of work you may consider doing and how to approach it. There are a number of textbooks and booklets available that concentrate on coursework, listed in Appendix A.

Teacher activity 12.1

Discuss the options for the assessment for practical skills with colleagues, considering both the available facilities and the course requirements.

Coursework

Teachers are not allowed to undertake school-based assessment without the written approval of the examination board. This approval is only given to teachers who satisfy examination board requirements concerning moderation. Teachers gain this approval by undergoing special training on assessment. Schools are offered in-service training at the examination board's headquarters or elsewhere, or via distance training packs. Courses delivered via the Internet are now becoming more common.

The process of moderation is a very important one. The teacher responsible for marking the students' assessments must be able to mark all the pieces of work to the same standard, using a mark scheme that has been supplied or that the teacher has devised. Samples of work with a range of marks are then sent to an external moderator, who makes sure that the marking is precise and fair and is comparable to standards in other schools and examination centres. The external moderator may change the marks awarded if they are judged too generous or too hard.

The skills that coursework is used to test vary from one examination board to another, but tend to include:

- using and organising techniques, apparatus and materials;
- observing, measuring and recording;
- handling experimental observations and data;
- planning investigations.

CIE publishes a manual called *IGCSE Science – assessment of practical skills* to support teachers who opt for coursework. It contains information and guidance about:

- each of the practical skills tested;
- choosing tasks for assessment;
- writing worksheets and mark schemes;
- details of the administration involved;
- marking each skill, providing marked examples with comments.

Other examination boards also produce books and manuals containing advice and examples of coursework, both marked (with a commentary to explain why marks have or have not been awarded) and unmarked so that teachers can compare the standard of their own marking with that of the examination board. Books from different examination boards are very useful, not only to show how to mark work, but also to provide ideas about which practicals are suitable for assessment. A range of suitable books is given in Appendix A.

Why do coursework?

- Teachers feel that they are more in control of their students' achievement, since they can guide students through the process, repeating it if students need to improve.

- You can give students feedback about their performance in an assessment. They can then work on weak areas in future submissions, gaining skills throughout the course.
- In opting for coursework, you can choose the topics your students are to be assessed on and you can develop your own teaching materials and mark schemes to support the assessment process.
- Gaining the skills required to moderate your students' coursework is an important part of a teacher's professional development.
- From the student's point of view, the coursework option means one less formal examination at the end of the course (practical examinations can be stressful for some).
- Students should also have a good idea of the mark they have gained before sitting their theory examinations, giving them more self-confidence if they have done well.

What are the disadvantages of the coursework option?
- You have to have written approval of the examination board, which is gained by being trained – as explained at the beginning of the chapter.
- You have to mark all the students' work, which can be time-consuming, and you have to keep records of the marks awarded for the external moderator. You are required to keep the work on file and this, or a sample, will have to be sent to the external moderator, who will check your marking.
- If there is more than one teaching set producing coursework for more than one teacher, your school needs to carry out internal moderation to make sure all teachers are marking to the same standard.
- Students can end up doing coursework in a large number of subjects, which is very time-consuming and can result in them becoming overloaded.

Practising coursework
Coursework can be practised (using a different topic on each occasion). This may be very time-consuming – you need to have strict time limits for each part of the process (e.g. 'You have one lesson to prepare a rough draft of your plan', having discussed the topic with the class). Some students panic – not knowing where to start. Checklists or writing frames may help (see Appendix D for examples). Stress the importance of individual work: even though students may need to share equipment, the planning, analysis, concluding and evaluating must be the student's own work.

It is not necessary to tackle all areas of assessment in one practical when developing these skills. One session may concentrate on the plan only. For another, you could provide the class with a plan that they all have to follow to collect a set of results. On another occasion, give them a set of results, having put it in context, from which they can draw conclusions. This book will provide you with examples of data you could use, but also keep copies of data collected by your classes. This is particularly useful for those students whose experiments have not gone to plan, perhaps resulting in an incomplete set of results (or none at all). They can still go through the formative process of handling data, plotting graphs and writing conclusions using other data. This sort of work does not have to be done in a laboratory – it makes very appropriate homework. The more opportunities students have to plan investigations, analyse data, plot graphs and form conclusions, the better they will become at these skills. You can even provide a class with copies of a previous student's work (remove any identifying features to keep it anonymous) along with the examination board criteria and instruct them to mark it. This will develop their familiarity with the criteria towards which they are working.

Practical test

This is usually a one-hour examination, carried out in examination conditions. The school is sent a list of requirements for the practical in advance of the examination and students require laboratory facilities to undergo the test.

Why opt for the practical test?
- The process of testing is complete after the examination. All the papers are sent to the examination board to be marked – that is not your responsibility, so it is less time-consuming than coursework.
- You do not have to be trained to enter your students for the practical test.
- The process is less time-consuming than coursework, although your students obviously need plenty of practical experience to perform well in the test.

What are the disadvantages of the practical test?
- An examination of this type can be very stressful for some students, who may not perform at their best in such a formal setting due to nervousness.
- Your school has to have sufficient resources and laboratory facilities to run the test. Good technical support is very important.
- The questions that come up in the test are beyond your control, whereas you can choose assessment material for coursework.
- Your students have to perform within a fixed time limit. This can be very challenging for some.

Alternative to practical

This paper is designed for schools that do not have the resources or facilities to carry out the practical test. Questions on the paper require students to demonstrate their familiarity with laboratory procedures, such as describing how to carry out a practical, drawing diagrams, measuring, processing data, drawing conclusions, selecting equipment and suggesting improvements to a technique or procedure.

Why opt for the alternative to practical?

Most of the reasons are similar to those for the practical test, but also:

- Large numbers of students can sit the examination at the same time (with the practical test, a number of sessions may have to be run consecutively).

What are the disadvantages of the alternative to practical?

Again, disadvantages are similar to those for the practical test, but also:

- Students will not have the opportunity to demonstrate (and therefore not gain merit for) some of the practical skills they may have learned.

Teacher activity 12.2

Even if your school enters your students for the practical test or the alternative to practical, it is important that they develop the skills and abilities listed in the coursework section of the syllabus. Choose the title of an investigation to set your class (preferably linked to a topic you have recently completed). Prepare all the supporting material that will provide guidance (planning sheets etc.) and decide on the range of resources (materials and apparatus) that will be needed. Also, plan how many lessons you will need to spend on the investigation and prepare an introductory lesson to provide background information and to set the task. The process will not only help your students to improve their practical skills, but also enable them to develop a better understanding of the topic.

Assessing students' work

Whichever form of assessment you opt to use, it is very important that your students have ample opportunity to develop their practical skills during the course and that they get feedback on the quality of work they are producing. You may choose to run some practicals in an examination setting, with your students organised differently from usual and maintaining strict rules about examination behaviour (no talking, no books or mobile phones etc.). You would then mark the work as if it was produced for the examination and give it back to the students with appropriate annotation (comments about where standards for a mark have been met, features missing and so on). I put this on my students' work in pencil in the margin, with a total (or totals depending on the areas being assessed) at the top of the work. You could use checklists such as those in Appendix D or produce your own mark scheme and provide your students with copies of this.

Do not be afraid of students challenging your marking, as long as it is justified. It is possible at times to overlook marking points that are creditworthy. A challenge shows a student is thinking about the criteria for marks. It may be that there is some evidence for the mark in question, but not quite enough. The challenge will help to identify what the student needs to do to gain that mark in future.

If you are entering students for the practical test or the alternative to practical, it is important to run a mock examination a few months before the real examination, so that students can experience the formality and challenges of the test. This takes organisation but is well worth doing. Students will then appreciate the importance of working independently, to strict time limits. Most schools use a past examination paper for this purpose. Do keep copies in a file, along with other information provided by the examination board, such as lists of apparatus required and guidelines about labelling of materials etc. Some specimens that have been used in previous examinations may be suitable for storage for future examinations (seeds, teeth and so on). This will make life easier for you and your technician. Again, mark the work and annotate it to provide feedback on strengths and weaknesses.

Examination boards publish mark schemes, so collect these and keep them with the examination papers. Principal examiners also produce reports on each examination. These are sent out to all schools following that syllabus. It will be very helpful for you to read these to identify common mistakes, variations between centres and so on. Spend a lesson after the mock examination going over the work, question by question. Identify common problems (do not keep targeting the same students when identifying these – you need to boost confidence rather than run the risk of making individuals feel they are failures). Discuss ways of improving the quality of work with the class. Ask them what they found most difficult or stressful and develop strategies to overcome these problems. Highlight the techniques used by the most successful students so that others can emulate them.

The timing of lessons can be a problem if you are trying to run a practical under examination conditions. Practical examinations tend to be an hour long. My lessons are only fifty minutes, so I could not run a full practical test without disrupting another lesson (and the laboratory needs to be free for at least an hour beforehand to allow sufficient time to set out all the materials). One way round this is to run parts of the practical in different lessons. Usually the practical consists of three different exercises, each of which could be set on different occasions. The same applies to alternative-to-practical papers and, of course, these could be set as homework to develop students' experience of the questions in this type of paper.

Do keep practical work in context, so that your students understand the background to what they are investigating, have sufficient knowledge to know what variables are involved and are able to draw appropriate conclusions. Provide feedback about the quality of work produced, identifying how it could be improved. Give your students copies of the criteria for the assessment of experimental skills and abilities (these can be photocopied from the syllabus), so that they know the standards required to achieve high marks.

LOOKING BACK

Practical skills are a very important part of any Science course and students are assessed on these.

♦ Do your students have sufficient opportunity to practise their practical skills? If not, how could you make more time available or improve the opportunities they do have?

♦ Are your students aware of the criteria on which they will be assessed? How could you help them to identify areas where they need to improve?

13 Conclusion

I hope that this book has challenged you to think about how much practical work you use in your teaching, the reasons for using it and ways of overcoming difficult issues associated with incorporating practical work into a teaching course. I am sure that you will agree that the advantages of practical work by far outweigh the disadvantages. As you use practical work more to support your teaching, your students' skills will develop rapidly. Not only will they become more competent at handling apparatus and become more self-confident, but they will develop a much better understanding of scientific concepts through their active involvement and their enjoyment of the subject will increase.

As you reflect more on the way that you teach, you will be able to identify your own needs for professional development. As teachers we never cease to learn. Ask for the support of colleagues, discuss ideas to develop alternative strategies and consider becoming involved in the process of examining. Try out teaching and learning styles that I have discussed in this book or that other teachers you work with find successful. If they do not work for you, then use others: I know of teachers who use drama very effectively in their teaching of Science, but I do not have the confidence to use it effectively, so I use other strategies. When starting a new topic, plan out the practical content and look for new ideas (perhaps from this book or from others – even old books!). If you find some useful alternative approaches make a note of the source or keep a file of photocopied pages for easier reference later. When you create a new worksheet, keep a copy on file to save having to rewrite it in the future.

I hope that you have the opportunity to try out some of the activities I have suggested with your students and that they find them worthwhile. Scientific investigation is about trial and error. So is teaching. Do not be afraid to try out new ideas. They may not all work, but if some do then you have gained – and so have your students.

Appendix A: useful sources of information

Some of the books listed may be out of print, but they are still useful. Examination boards such as CIE now endorse textbooks that match their syllabuses and I have included these. However, when looking for ideas for practical work, nearly all Science textbooks will provide you with some, and each author will have some suggestions that are different from the standard experiments with which most of us are familiar. Do not be put off skimming through a textbook just because it is old or out of print.

If you have difficulty getting to a bookshop, you could consider buying online. Internet booksellers such as Amazon.com may be helpful. Many publishers also have facilities for online ordering of books.

Books concentrating on practical work

Beckett, B., Bethell, G. and Crowther, B. (1996) *Coordinated Science Chemistry: teachers' guide*, Oxford University Press

Beckett, B., Bethell, G. and Crowther, B. (1996) *Coordinated Science Physics: teachers' guide*, Oxford University Press

Beckett, B., Gallagher, R. M., Ingram, P. and Pople, S. (1996), *Coordinated Science Biology: teachers' guide*, Oxford University Press

Byers, A., Childs, A. and Laine, C. (1994) *The Science teachers' handbook*, VSO

Clegg, A. (1996) *Chemistry for IGCSE: a teacher's guide*, Heinemann International

Freeland, P. (1987) *Investigations for GCSE Biology* Hodder and Stoughton

Goldsworthy, A., Watson, J.R. and Wood-Robinson, V. (2000) *Developing understanding* and *Getting to grips with graphs*, Association for Science Education

Green, N. P. O., Stout, G. W., Taylor, D.J. and Soper, R. (1997) *Biological Science 1 & 2*, Cambridge University Press

Hardy, J. and Tranter, J. (1983) *Biology practicals*, Addison-Wesley

Hunt, A. and Sykes, A. (1984) *Chemistry*, Longman

Jerram, A. (2000) *Teaching Physics to KS4*, Hodder and Stoughton Educational

Jones, M. (1994) *Biology for IGCSE: teacher's guide*, Heinemann

McDuell, B. (2002) *Teaching secondary Chemistry*, John Murray (ASE)

Pickering, W. (2000) *Complete Biology*, Oxford University Press

Pruden, V. (1999) *Assessing Sc1 for GCSE*, Heinemann

Reis, M. (ed.) (1999) *Teaching secondary Biology*, John Murray (ASE)

Sang, D. (ed.) (2002) *Teaching secondary Physics*, John Murray (ASE)

Sang, D. and Wood-Robinson, V. (eds.) (2002) *Teaching scientific enquiry*, John Murray (ASE)

Endorsed textbooks

Duncan, T. and Kennett, H. (2002) *IGCSE Physics*, John Murray (ASE)

Earl, B. and Wilford, L. (2002) *IGCSE Chemistry*, John Murray (ASE)

Harwood, R. (2002) *Chemistry – New Edition*, Cambridge University Press

Jones, M. (2003) *O Level Biology*, Oxford University Press

Jones, M. and Jones, G. (2002) *Biology – International Edition for IGCSE and O Level*, Cambridge University Press

Jones, M. (2002) *Biology for IGCSE*, new edition, Heinemann

Mackean, D. (2002) *IGCSE Biology*, John Murray (ASE)

Other publications

Assessment and Qualifications Alliance (2002) *Success with Science coursework*

Association for Science Education (1996) *Safeguards in the school laboratory*

Association for Science Education (1995) *Signs, symbols and systematics: the ASE companion to 5–16 Science*

Cambridge International Examinations (2002) *Planning for practical Science in secondary schools*

Institute of Biology (2000) *Biological nomenclature, standard terms and expressions used in the teaching of Biology*

University of Cambridge Local Examinations Syndicate (UCLES) (2000) *IGCSE Science – assessment of practical skills*

University of Cambridge Local Examinations Syndicate (UCLES) (1998) *IGCSE standards in Biology/Chemistry/Physics*

CD-ROMs

Alchemy?, Royal Society of Chemistry (www.rsc.org)

ASE Science Year resources, Association for Science Education (www.ase.org.uk)

Chemistry set 2000, New Media Press Ltd (www.new-media.co.uk)

Crocodile clips Chemistry, Crocodile clips Physics, Crocodile Clips Ltd (www.crocodile-clips.com)

PRI – ideas and evidence, Collins (www.CollinsEducation.com)

RSC electronic data book, Royal Society of Chemistry (www.rsc.org)

Understanding electricity: sources of energy, Electricity Association Services Ltd (www.electricity.org.uk)

Professional associations

Association for Science Education
College Lane, Hatfield, Herts AL10 9AA
Tel: +44 (0)1707 283000; Fax: +44 (0)1707 266532
www.ase.org.uk

Institute of Biology
20 Queensbury Place, London SW7 2DZ
Tel: +44 (0)20 7581 8333; Fax: +44 (0)20 7823 9409
www.iob.org

Institute of Physics
76 Portland Place, London W1B 1NT
Tel: +44 (0)20 7470 4800; Fax: +44 (0)20 7470 4848
www.iop.org

Royal Society of Chemistry
Burlington House, Piccadilly, London W1J 0BA
Tel: +44 (0)20 7437 8656; Fax: +44 (0)20 7437 8883
www.rsc.org

A comprehensive list of chemistry societies can be found at
www.chemsoc.org/societies/society1.htm

Other useful websites

• www.cie.org.uk – Cambridge International Examinations (CIE) offers
an increasing number of opportunities to teachers in the area of
professional development. This book is part of CIE's commitment in this
area. Do investigate what is now available and consider how these can
benefit you in terms of professional development and the quality of your
teaching skills.
• www.cleapss.org.uk – **CLEAPSS School Science Service** provides
schools (teachers and technicians) with up-to-date information about safe
practice, management, equipment and the handling and storing of
chemicals. They run courses and publish materials for schools.
• www.shu.ac.uk/pri – the **Pupil Researcher Initiative** (PRI) website,
set up and run by the Pupil Researcher Initiative at Sheffield Hallam
University, provides Pupil Briefs for investigations, with secondary
sources and background reading in new real life contexts. A dedicated
investigation site (www.sci-journal.org/index.php?c_check=1) publishes
students' reports.
• www.saps.plantsci.cam.ac.uk – **Science and Plants for Schools**
(SAPS) is a charity that has the aim of encouraging and supporting
interesting and lively teaching. It develops ideas, based on plant science
and molecular biology, from teachers and from research scientists to
provide resources that work in the classroom. These resources include
information, for example in the form of worksheets, about investigations
into various aspects of plant science. It also provides links to other sites
that may provide useful ideas to enhance your teaching.
• www.sep.org.uk – the **Science Enhancement Programme** (SEP) is
a Gatsby-funded organisation that provides practical kits and web-based
resources. They also supply a very cheap and easy-to-use data logger
called *ibutton*, which measures temperature.

Appendix B: glossary

accuracy	the precision with which an instrument is used in measuring
assessment	measurement of how effectively students have learned, usually by reference to stated learning outcomes
assessment objectives	the criteria that need to be met to demonstrate effective learning
audit	an examination of the resources present in, for example, a department
checklist	a reference list used by students to make sure they have completed all tasks in an assessment
concept	an abstract idea
Coordinated Science	a Science course that includes Biology, Chemistry and Physics
coursework	practical assessment work completed under supervision in class that may contribute to a student's final examination mark
criteria	set of standards against which assessment can be measured
curriculum	programmes of learning and those factors which influence the quality of learning
data logging	a process of automatic data capturing and recording
demonstration	teaching strategy where students are shown a particular technique that they may then practise
departmental policy	agreed procedures followed by all subject teachers
discussion	teaching strategy where students are encouraged to talk to each other about a particular topic and report back
evaluation	critical review of an investigation through careful analysis of data and conclusion
feedback	informing the student of their ability in a particular task

formative assessment	type of assessment to help with teaching and learning and how a student can improve their performance
investigation	a complete experiment that involves planning, collecting data, analysing the results and evaluating
objective	short-term target
question and answer	teaching strategy where the teacher asks a question and the student responds; can also be used as an assessment technique
reliability	the extent to which results can be trusted
scheme of work	an outline of a teaching sequence to cover the contents of a syllabus, usually including teaching objectives, timings, resources and homework suggestions
strategy	plan of action
summative assessment	type of assessment used at the end of a teaching programme; one such example is any external examination used for certification purposes
syllabus	an outline of a course of study, published by an Examination Board
validity	the soundness of a judgement
variables	factors in an experiment that are not constant unless controlled
writing frame	a series of questions provided to help students structure an investigation

Appendix C: lists of apparatus

The particular apparatus found in a Science department will be determined by a large number of factors including the number of laboratories, the size of the school, the number and size of teaching sets being taught at the same time, as well as the level of funding. The lists of apparatus in this appendix are taken from CIE (2002).

Biology
Standard apparatus
A means of heating – Bunsen burners or similar
A means of measuring small volumes (e.g. syringes of various sizes)
A means of writing on glassware (e.g. water-resistant markers)
Beakers
Benedict's solution
Biuret reagent/potassium hydroxide and copper sulphate solution
Black paper/aluminium foil
Bungs to fit some test tubes/boiling tubes
Conical flasks and clamp stands (for specific experiments)
Cotton wool
Cutting implement (e.g. solid-edged razor blade/knife/scalpel)
Equipment to make potometer
Ethanol (for fats test)
Filter funnels and filter paper
Forceps
Glass slides and coverslips
Glucose
Hand lenses (not less than ×6, preferably ×8)
Iodine solution
Measuring cylinders
Methylated spirit (extraction of chlorophyll)
Microscope and lamp
Mounted needles
Paper towelling or tissue
Petri dishes (plastic) or similar small containers
Potassium hydroxide
Safety spectacles
Scissors
Sodium chloride
Solid glass rods

Specimen tubes with corks
Starch
Sucrose
Teat pipettes
Test tubes and boiling tubes
Test tube holders or similar means of holding tubes
Test tube racks or similar in which to stand tubes
Thermometers
Visking tubing
White tile or other suitable surface on which to cut

Desirable apparatus
Copper sulphate (crystals)
Dilute hydrochloric acid
Distilled/deionised water
Eosin/red ink
Hydrogencarbonate indicator
Limewater
Litmus paper
Methylene blue
Mortars and pestles
Sodium bicarbonate
Universal indicator paper and chart
Vaseline/petroleum jelly (or similar)

Chemistry
The following lists do not include items that are commonly regarded as standard equipment (such as burners, tripods, glass tubing) but instead lists the specific equipment required for teaching at IGCSE/O Level. A complete list of chemicals is not given as this will depend on the experiments taught but a list of the common bench reagents required is given.

Specific equipment
Beaker, squat form with lip: 250 cm^3
Boiling tubes, approximately 150 mm $\times$ 25 mm
Burette, 50 cm^3
Clocks (or wall-clock) to measure to an accuracy of about 1 second
Conical flasks within the range 150 cm^3 to 250 cm^3
Filter funnel
Measuring cylinder, 50 cm^3 or 25 cm^3
Pipette, 25 cm^3
Pipette filler

Polystyrene or plastic beaker of approximate capacity 150 cm^3
Stirring rod
Test tubes (some of which should be Pyrex or hard glass),
   approximately 125 mm $\times$ 16 mm
Thermometer, $-10\ °C$ to $110\ °C$ at $1\ °C$ intervals
Wash bottle

Standard bench reagents
Aqueous ammonia (approximately 1.0 mol/dm^3)
Aqueous barium nitrate or aqueous barium chloride
   (approximately 0.2 mol/dm^3)
Aqueous lead(II) nitrate (approximately 0.2 mol/dm^3)
Aqueous potassium dichromate(VI) (approximately 0.1 mol/dm^3)
Aqueous potassium iodide (approximately 0.1 mol/dm^3)
Aqueous potassium manganate(VII) (approximately 0.02 mol/dm^3)
Aqueous silver nitrate (approximately 0.05 mol/dm^3)
Aqueous sodium hydroxide (approximately 1.0 mol/dm^3)
Hydrochloric acid (approximately 1.0 mol/dm^3)
Limewater (a saturated solution of calcium hydroxide)
Nitric acid (approximately 1.0 mol/dm^3)
Sulphuric acid (approximately 0.5 mol/dm^3)

Other material
Aluminium foil
Red and blue litmus paper or universal indicator paper

Note: For testing carbon dioxide, delivery tubes are not necessary. If these are unavailable, students can either pour the gas carefully into a test tube containing limewater and shake, or use a bulb pipette to sample the gas and bubble it through some limewater in a test tube.

Physics
The following lists are not intended to be exhaustive, but do give an indication of the apparatus used in the various practical examinations of CIE's Physics syllabuses.

General apparatus
12 V, 24 W filament bulb
Ammeter, 1 A or 1.5 A
Beakers, 100 cm^3, 250 cm^3, 1 litre
Blu-tack
Boiling tube, 150 mm $\times$ 25 mm
Stiff white card

Cells, 1.5 V
Connecting leads
Crocodile clips
DC power supply, variable to 12 V
G-clamp
Half-metre rule
Lens, converging, $f = 15$ cm
Low voltage (2.5 V) filament bulbs and holders
Masses, 50 g and 100 g
Measuring cylinders, 100 cm^3 and 250 cm^3
Metre rule
Microscope slides
Mirror, plane, 50 mm $\times$ 10 mm
Nichrome wire, 28 swg (0.38 mm diameter) and 30 swg (0.32 mm diameter)
Pendulum bob
Pin board
Pivot (to fit a hole in metre rule)
Plastic or polystyrene cup, 200 cm^3
Plasticene
Protractor
Resistors, various
Retort stand, boss and clamp
Sellotape
Spring balance, 0.5 N to 1.0 N
Springs
Stopwatch, reading to 0.1 s or better
Switch
Thermometer, -10 °C to 110 °C at 1 °C intervals
Thread
Tracing paper
Voltmeter, full scale deflection 1 V and 5 V
Wooden board

Note: Digital multimeters often provide a cheap and flexible alternative to a range of ammeters and voltmeters.

Physics departments vary a great deal in the apparatus available for teaching. Many of the items listed for the practical examinations can be used, with some imagination, to support the teaching of IGCSE, O Level and A Level Physics and as the basis for IGCSE coursework tasks. Physics equipment is also expensive and this will almost certainly be a factor. The following is offered as outline guidance for the sorts of apparatus that centres may wish to consider for teaching purposes.

Mechanics
Free-fall apparatus
Power supplies
Ticker timers
Trolleys
Runways

Energy
Electric motor
Energy conversion kit
Joulemeter

Heat and properties of matter
Marbles and a tray, or kinetic model apparatus
Springs and mass sets
Thermometers of various types

Electricity
Electroscope or other apparatus for illustrating simple electrostatic phenomena, for example nylon, perspex and ebonite rods
Different diameters of wire of different materials (copper, constantan, nichrome etc.)
Set of apparatus for circuit work: cells, voltmeters, ammeters, variable and fixed resistors, lamps, diodes, thermistors, switches etc.

It is important to choose meter ranges that are appropriate for the power supplies and resistors used.

Magnetism
Electromagnet
Magnets, bar and horseshoe
Motor kits or apparatus to demonstrate Fleming's left-hand rule
Plotting compasses, iron filings
Transformer or apparatus to demonstrate electromagnetic induction

Waves
Microphone and cathode-ray oscilloscope
Ray boxes, glass blocks (rectangular and semi-circular), pins
Ripple tank
Rope, 'Slinky' spring
Signal generator and loudspeaker

Microwave apparatus and a laser are good extras.

Modern Physics

Radioactive sources, detectors and absorbers

Teltron tubes, EHT power supply and apparatus for deflection by electric and magnetic fields

Much of the apparatus for this work is expensive and access to some items may be restricted by local regulations. Videos or computer simulations may prove adequate substitutes.

Appendix D: photocopiable worksheets

The worksheets reproduced here are A5 size. They are designed to be enlarged through photocopying to A4 size for use by students.

Worksheet 1: Example of a planning checklist

Planning an investigation

Name _____

Form _____

Introduction

- [ ] Relevant information about the topic, from a textbook, *Encarta* etc.
- [ ] Keep the notes short (usually one paragraph)
- [ ] Make sure the notes are in **your** own words
- [ ] Include key words
- [ ] Use diagrams if possible, linked to your written information
- [ ] Make a note of the title of any book/software used for source material

Preliminary work

- [ ] Describe what experiment(s) you have done already about the topic
- [ ] State what you found out

Prediction

- [ ] State what you expect to happen
- [ ] Explain why – and link this with information in your introduction

Equipment list

- [ ] List of equipment
- [ ] Reasons for choosing equipment (refer to accuracy)

Instructions for carrying out your investigation

- [ ] Written in present or future tense
- [ ] Written step-by-step (can be with bullet points)
- [ ] Fair test included (what you will keep the same)
- [ ] Variable identified (what you will change each time)
- [ ] Include the range of readings you will take
- [ ] State how many repeats you will make
- [ ] Explain why you will take repeat readings
- [ ] Include safety points

Worksheet 2: Example of a writing frame for Chemistry

Planning an investigation

Rate of reaction investigation

Name _____

Form _____

What I am trying to find out:

_____

This is the apparatus I will use: (you can draw a labelled diagram)

_____
| |
| |
| |
| |
| |
| |
|_____|

The chemicals I will use are:

_____

The apparatus I will use to measure the volumes of the chemicals will be:

_____

I will make my investigation a fair test by keeping these things the same:

_____

The thing I will vary will be:

_____

The range for this variable will be:

_____

I know the reaction has finished when:

_____

I will time the reaction with:

_____

My prediction (what I expect to happen) is:

_____

The reason for my prediction is:

_____

Worksheet 3: Example of a writing frame for Physics

Planning an investigation
Current in a bulb

Name _____

Form _____

Your task is to investigate how the **voltage** across a bulb affects the **current** in it.

What **equipment** will you need?

_____

Draw a **circuit diagram** you could use.

What will you **change**?	What **values** will you us

What will you **measure**?

_____

How will you make sure it is **reliable**?

_____

How will you make sure it is a fair test?

_____

What **safety** precautions will you take?

_____

Worksheet 4a: Outline drawings of apparatus

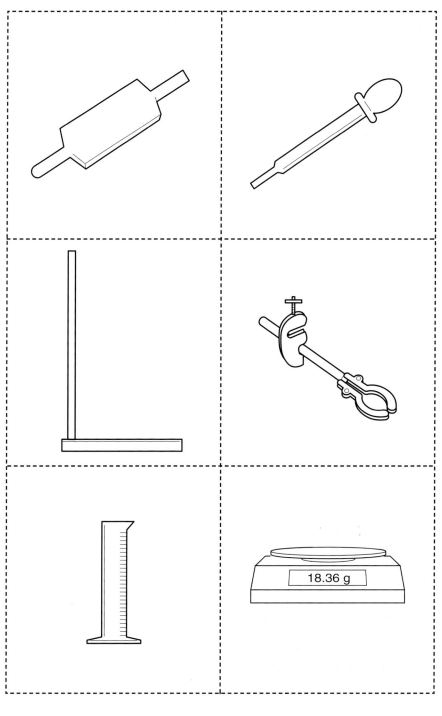

Worksheet 4b: Outline drawings of apparatus (continued)

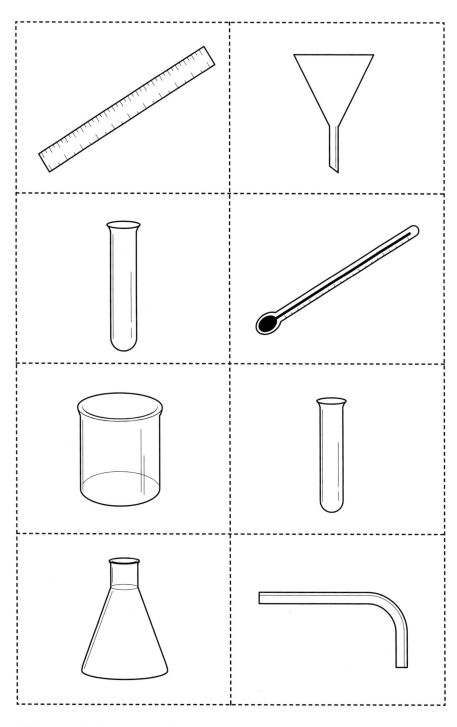

Worksheet 4c: Outline drawings of apparatus (continued)

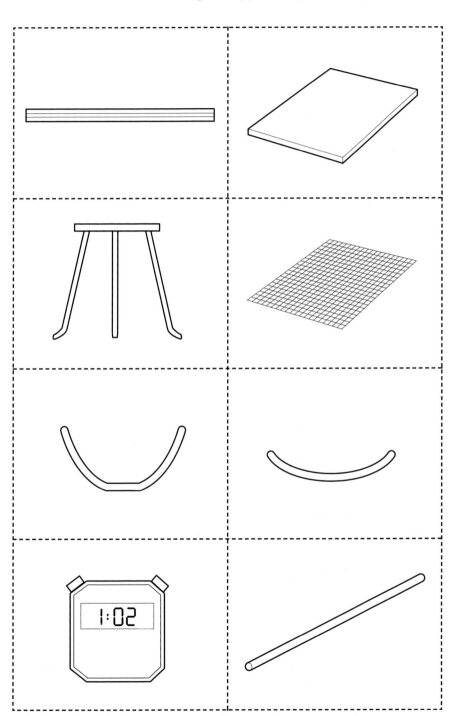

beaker	pipette
boiling tube	retort stand
boss and clamp	ruler
bung	stirring rod
capillary tubing	stopwatch
conical flask	test tube

delivery tube	test tube rack
evaporating dish	thermometer
funnel	tile
gauze	top pan balance
heatproof mat	tripod
measuring cylinder	watch glass

Worksheet 6: Example of an instruction sheet

Making a salt

You are to prepare a sample of hydrated magnesium sulphate crystals using dilute sulphuric acid and magnesium oxide. Use the following method.

1   Using a measuring cylinder, put 50 cm^3 of dilute sulphuric acid into a beaker. Warm the solution, but do not boil. Add the magnesium oxide in small portions, with stirring, until no more will dissolve.

2   Filter and discard the excess solid.

3   Evaporate the filtrate to crystallisation point and then allow to cool.

4   Collect the crystals either by filtration or by decantation and dry them by pressing gently between filter papers.

5   Put the crystals in a tube labelled with your name.

Worksheet 7a: Example of illustrated instructions

Preparing a slide of plant cells

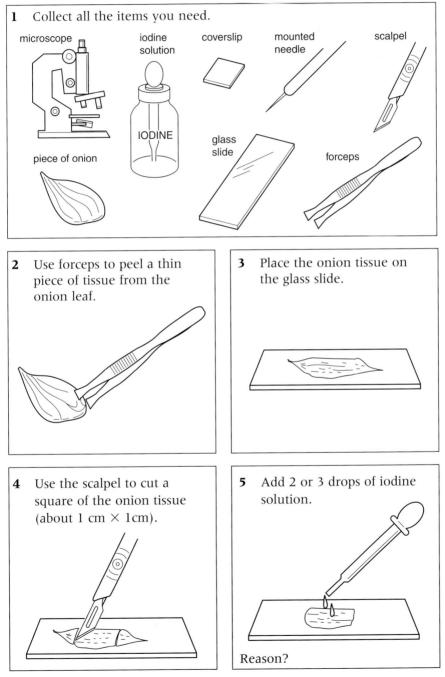

1 Collect all the items you need.

microscope
iodine solution
coverslip
mounted needle
scalpel
IODINE
glass slide
piece of onion
forceps

2 Use forceps to peel a thin piece of tissue from the onion leaf.

3 Place the onion tissue on the glass slide.

4 Use the scalpel to cut a square of the onion tissue (about 1 cm × 1cm).

5 Add 2 or 3 drops of iodine solution.

Reason?

Worksheet 7b: Example of illustrated instructions (continued)

Preparing a slide of plant cells (continued)

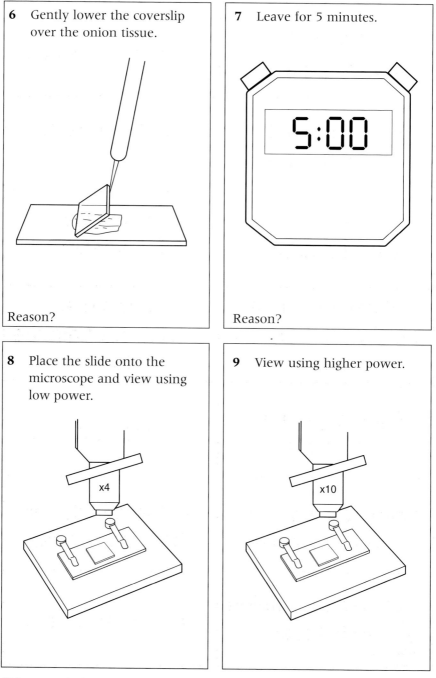

6 Gently lower the coverslip over the onion tissue.

Reason?

7 Leave for 5 minutes.

Reason?

8 Place the slide onto the microscope and view using low power.

x4

9 View using higher power.

x10

Worksheet 8: Sentence completion and sequencing cards

Starch test

Turn on the Bunsen burner	to heat the water.
Place the leaf in boiling water	to kill the leaf.
Turn off the Bunsen burner	alcohol is flammable.
Place the leaf in alcohol and allow it to boil	to remove chlorophyll from the leaf.
Put the leaf back into water	to soften the leaf.
Spread out the leaf on a white tile	so the results will be easy to see.
Add iodine solution to the leaf	to test for starch.

Worksheet 9: Laboratory safety rules

Laboratory Safety Rules

1 Pupils must **not** enter the laboratory unless there is a teacher present.

2 Report **all** accidents and breakages to the teacher.

3 You must **not** eat, drink or chew in the laboratory.

4 **Never** run or play in the laboratory.

5 Wear safety spectacles whenever advised to do so.

6 If you are not sure what to do, ask your teacher.

7 **Always** wash your hands at the end of an experiment.

8 Apparatus and materials must **not** be taken away from the laboratory.

9 Think about what you are doing and work safely at all times.

10 **Always** follow instructions completely and look out for dangers when carrying out experiments and working in the laboratory.

Worksheet 10: Analysing checklist

Investigation analysis

Name _____

Form _____

Graph

☐ Title for graph

☐ Graph axes drawn, using a pencil and ruler

☐ Controlled variable (the factor **you** change) is on the *x*-axis

☐ Appropriate scale used ('graph fills the page')

☐ Units for *x*- and *y*-axes

☐ Labels for *x*- and *y*-axes

☐ Points clearly plotted, with ⊙ or ✕

☐ Line of best fit (this **can** be a curve!)

☐ Check any calculations are correct

Conclusion

☐ Heading for conclusion

☐ Identify any trends shown in the results table

☐ State the relationship shown on the graph

☐ Link the relationship to the conclusion

☐ Compare your conclusion with your theory (re-state it)

☐ Use data from your graph to support your conclusion

Worksheet 11: Evaluation checklist

Investigation evaluation

Name _____

Form _____

- [ ] Comment on the quality of results shown by the graph
- [ ] Identify any anomalous (odd) results
- [ ] State any problems you had with your practical investigation
- [ ] Suggest how you improve it to get rid of these difficulties
- [ ] State if you collected repeat results
- [ ] State if the repeats were similar to the first set (and are therefore reliable)
- [ ] State what you did to make sure your results were accurate
- [ ] State, with reasons, how well your evidence supports your conclusion
- [ ] Give a detailed description of further work to get extra evidence
- [ ] Compare the results collected with secondhand evidence

Index

(A 't' next to a page number
   indicates a table; an 'f'
   indicates a figure.)

experiments and resulting
graphs 61t
observations, opportunities for
making 43t
writing frame 30, 100
pie charts 56–7
*Planning for practical Science in
secondary schools* (CIE booklet)
8, 38
practical skills 5, 23–5, 85
assessment of 78–84
practical tests 78, 81, 83
practical work 1–2, 5–9, 85
building understanding 36
planning Science course 10–22
praise, importance of 29
predicting skills 28
predictions
investigation 28–30
referring back to 67
problem set, referring back to 67
pulse rate, measurement 45

rate of reaction, effect of
concentration on 16t, 63–5,
73–4
reagents, working safely with 23
results
describing processed 62
reliable vs. accurate 27
using tables to record 49–52

safety
during practicals 28, 29
in laboratory 23, 32, 37–8, 110
Science Enhancement Programme
(SEP) 20
Science teachers' handbook 13
sentence completion cards 37
software packages 20
starch, testing leaf for 36
students

encouraging self-reliance 35
encouraging thinking and
understanding 36

tables
identifying faults in 52–3
using to record results 49–52
temperature
effect on rate of a reaction 68f
effect on time taken for a
reaction 67f
textbooks 2, 25

units, used in tables 51

variables
dependent (output) 30, 44, 52,
56
independent (input) 30, 44, 52,
56

video microscopes 21
volume, of irregular solids 12

worksheets 35, 37, 97–112
writing frames 30, 69, 77, 80, 99,
100

Other titles in the Professional Development for Teachers series